Teach & Test

Math Grade 1

Table of Contents

How to Use This Book

1. This book can be used in a home or classroom setting. Read through each unit before working with the student(s). Familiarize yourself with the vocabulary and the skills that are introduced at the top of each unit activity page. Use this information as a guide to help instruct the student(s).

2. Choose a quiet place with little or no interruptions (including the telephone). Talk with the student(s) about the purpose of this book and how you will be working as a team to prepare for standardized tests.

3. As an option, copy the unit test and give it as a pretest to identify weak areas.

4. Upon the completion of each unit, you will find a unit test. Discuss the Helping Hand strategy for test taking featured on the test. Use the example on each test as a chance to show the student(s) how to work through a problem and completely fill in the answer circle. Encourage the student(s) to work independently when possible, but this is a learning time and questions should be welcomed. A time limit is given for each test. Instruct the student(s) to use the time allowed efficiently, looking back over the answers if possible. Tell him to continue until he sees the stop sign.

5. Record the score on the record sheet on page 4. If a student has difficulty with any questions, use the cross-reference guide on the inside back cover to identify the skills that need to be reviewed.

Teach & Test

Introduction

now this makes sense—teaching our students the skills and strategies that are expected of them before they are tested!

Many students, parents, and teachers are concerned that standardized test scores do not adequately reflect a child's capabilities. This may be due to one or more of the factors italicized below. The purpose of this book is to reduce the negative impact of these, or similar factors, on a student's standardized test scores. The goal is to target those factors and alter their effects as described.

1. *The student has been taught the tested skills but has forgotten them.* This book is divided into units that are organized similarly to first grade textbooks. Instructions for the skill itself are found at the top of each unit activity page, ensuring that the student has been exposed to each key component. The exercises include drill/practice and creative learning activities. Additional activity suggestions can be found in a star burst within the units. These activities require the students to apply the skills that they are practicing.

2. *The student has mastered the skills but has never seen them presented in a test-type format.* Ideally, the skills a student learns at school will be used as part of problem solving in the outside world. For this reason, the skills in this book, and in most classrooms, are not practiced in a test-type format. At the end of each unit in this book, the skills are specifically matched with test questions. In this way, the book serves as a type of "bridge" between the skills that the student(s) has mastered and the standardized test format.

3. *The student is inexperienced with the answer sheet format.* Depending on the standardized test that your school district uses, students are expected to use a fill-in-the-bubble name grid and score sheet. To familiarize students with this process, a name grid and score sheet are included for the review tests found at the midway point and again at the end of the book.

4. *The student may feel the anxiety of a new and unfamiliar situation.* While testing, students will notice changes in their daily routine: their classroom door will be closed with a "Testing" sign on it, children will be asked not to use the restroom, their desks may be separated, their teacher may read from a script and refuse to repeat herself, etc. To help relieve the stress caused by these changes, treat each unit test in this book as it would be treated at school by following the procedures listed below.

Stage a Test

You will find review tests midway through the book and again at the end of the book. When you reach these points, "stage a test" by creating a real test-taking environment. The procedures listed below coincide with many standardized test directions. The purpose is to alleviate stress, rather than contribute to it, so make this a serious, but calm, event and the student(s) will benefit.

1. Prepare! Have the student(s) sharpen two pencils, lay out scratch paper, and use the restroom.

2. Choose a room with a door that can be closed. Ask a student to put a sign on the door that reads "Testing" and explain that no talking will be permitted after the sign is hung.

3. Direct the student(s) to turn to a specific page but not to begin until the instructions are completely given.

4. Read the instructions at the top of the page and work through the example together. Discuss the Helping Hand strategy that is featured at the top of the page. Have the student(s) neatly and completely fill in the bubble for the example. This is the child's last chance to ask for help!

5. Instruct the student(s) to continue working until the stop sign is reached. If a student needs help reading, you may read each question only once.

Helping Hand Test Strategies

The first page of each test features a specific test-taking strategy that will be helpful in working through most standardized tests. These strategies are introduced and spotlighted one at a time so that they will be learned and remembered internally. Each will serve as a valuable test-taking tool, so discuss them thoroughly.

The strategies include:

- Always read or listen to each question carefully.
- Read all of the choices before you answer.
- With picture answers, cover some of the choices so you see only one picture at a time.
- Find your own answer before reading the choices.
- When using scratch paper, copy carefully.
- Compare the answer choices. Some may look very similar.
- Use your time wisely. If a problem seems tough, skip it and come back to it later.
- Read the question again. Does your answer make sense?

Constructed-Response Questions

You will find the final question of each test is written in a different format called constructed response. This means that students are not provided with answer choices, but are instead asked to construct their own answers. The objective of such an "open-ended" type of question is to provide students with a chance to creatively develop reasonable answers. It also provides an insight to a student's reasoning and thinking skills. As this format is becoming more accepted and encouraged by standardized test developers, students will be "ahead of the game" by practicing such responses now.

Evaluating the Tests

Two types of questions are included in each test. The unit tests and the midway review test consist of 20 multiple-choice questions, and the final review test consists of 30 multiple-choice questions. All tests include a "constructed-response" question which requires the student(s) to construct and sometimes support an answer. Use the following procedures to evaluate a student's performance on each test.

1. Use the answer key found on pages 126–128 to correct the tests. Be sure the student(s) neatly and completely filled in the answer circles.

2. Record the scores on the record sheet found on page 4. If the student(s) incorrectly answered any questions, use the cross-reference guide found on the inside back cover to help identify the skills the student(s) needs to review. Each test question references the corresponding activity page.

3. Scoring the "constructed-response" questions is somewhat subjective. Discuss these questions with the student(s). Sometimes it is easier for the student(s) to explain the answer verbally. Help the student to record his thoughts as a written answer. If the student(s) has difficulty formulating a response, refer back to the activity pages using the cross-reference guide. Also review the star burst activity found in the unit which also requires the student(s) to formulate an answer.

4. Discuss the test with the student(s). What strategies were used to answer the questions? Were some questions more difficult than others? Was there enough time? What strategies did the student(s) use while taking the test?

Record Sheet

Record a student's score for each test by drawing a star or placing a sticker below each item number that was correct. Leave the incorrect boxes empty as this will allow you to visually see any weak spots. Review and practice those missed skills, then retest only the necessary items.

Unit 1

1	2	3	4	5	6	7	8	9	10	11	12	13	14	15	16	17	18	19	20

Unit 2

1	2	3	4	5	6	7	8	9	10	11	12	13	14	15	16	17	18	19	20

Unit 3

1	2	3	4	5	6	7	8	9	10	11	12	13	14	15	16	17	18	19	20

Unit 4

1	2	3	4	5	6	7	8	9	10	11	12	13	14	15	16	17	18	19	20

Midway Review Test

1	2	3	4	5	6	7	8	9	10	11	12	13	14	15	16	17	18	19	20

Unit 5

1	2	3	4	5	6	7	8	9	10	11	12	13	14	15	16	17	18	19	20

Unit 6

1	2	3	4	5	6	7	8	9	10	11	12	13	14	15	16	17	18	19	20

Unit 7

1	2	3	4	5	6	7	8	9	10	11	12	13	14	15	16	17	18	19	20

Unit 8

1	2	3	4	5	6	7	8	9	10	11	12	13	14	15	16	17	18	19	20

Final Review Test

1	2	3	4	5	6	7	8	9	10	11	12	13	14	15	16	17	18	19	20

21	22	23	24	25	26	27	28	29	30

Name

Counting to 20   Unit 1

This is a **number line**. It shows numbers from 0 to 20 in counting order.

```
←——|——|——|——|——|——|——|——|——|——|——|——|——|——|——|——|——|——|——|——|——|——→
    0  1  2  3  4  5  6  7  8  9 10 11 12 13 14 15 16 17 18 19 20
```

Write the numbers from **1** to **20** on the baseball caps. Write them again on the back of each jersey.

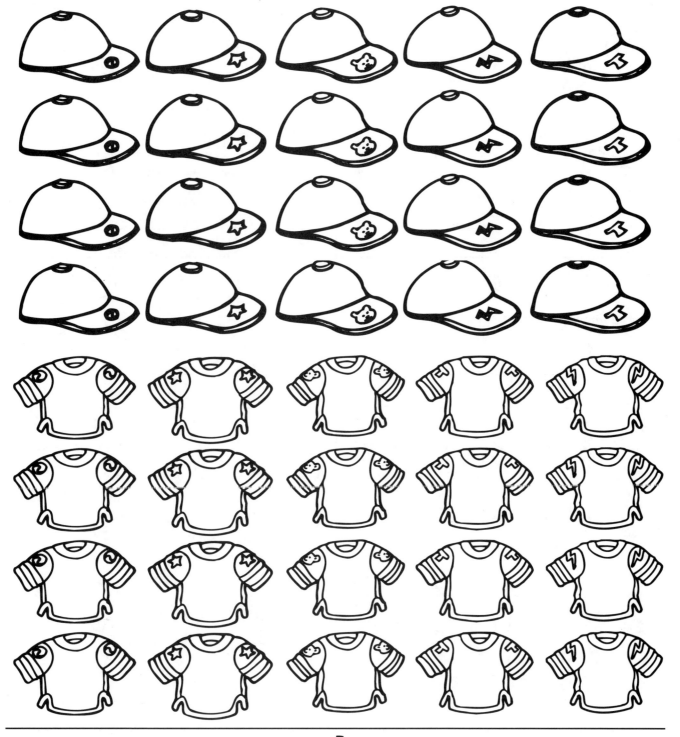

Name

Counting objects to 20   Unit 1

Counting objects is easier when you make a small pencil mark on each object as you count it. That way, you will always know which ones have been counted.

Count. Write the number.

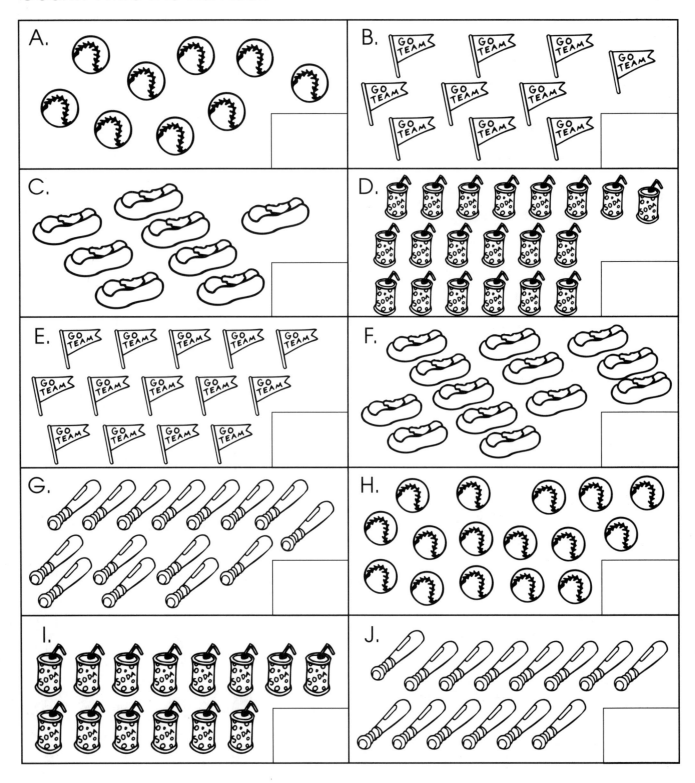

Name

Sequencing

Unit 1

A **sequence** is a certain order. To find a sequence, you must carefully read the directions.

Sequence the pictures by writing **1**, **2**, **3**, and **4** to show the order.

A. biggest to smallest

____   ____   ____   ____

B. tallest to shortest

____   ____   ____   ____

C. smallest to largest

____   ____   ____   ____

D. most to fewest

____   ____   ____   ____

E. largest to smallest

____   ____   ____   ____

F. fewest to most

____   ____   ____   ____

Name

Ordinal numbers

When numbers are sequenced, their names change: 1 is called first (1st), 2 is called second (2nd), 3 is called third (3rd), and so on.

Color the birds, bugs, and flowers:

1st = blue	2nd = yellow	3rd = green
4th = purple	5th = red	6th = orange
7th = pink	8th = brown	9th = black

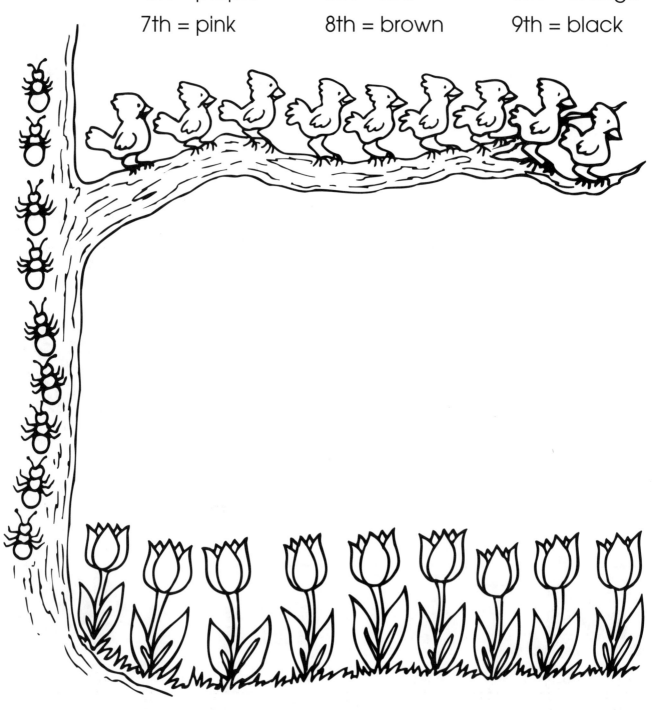

Name

Counting to 100   Unit 1

Did you know that numbers never end? Luckily, they follow a pattern that makes it fun to count on and on.

Complete the chart. Write the numbers from **1** to **100**.

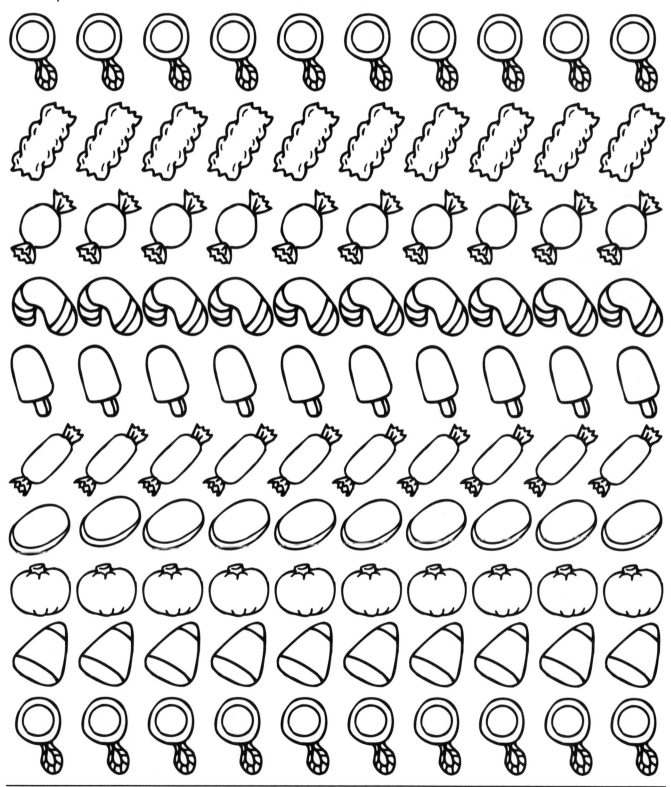

Name

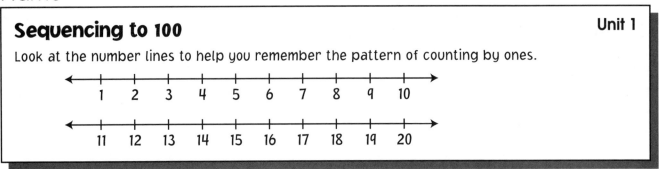

Sequencing to 100

Look at the number lines to help you remember the pattern of counting by ones.

1 2 3 4 5 6 7 8 9 10

11 12 13 14 15 16 17 18 19 20

Write the missing numbers.

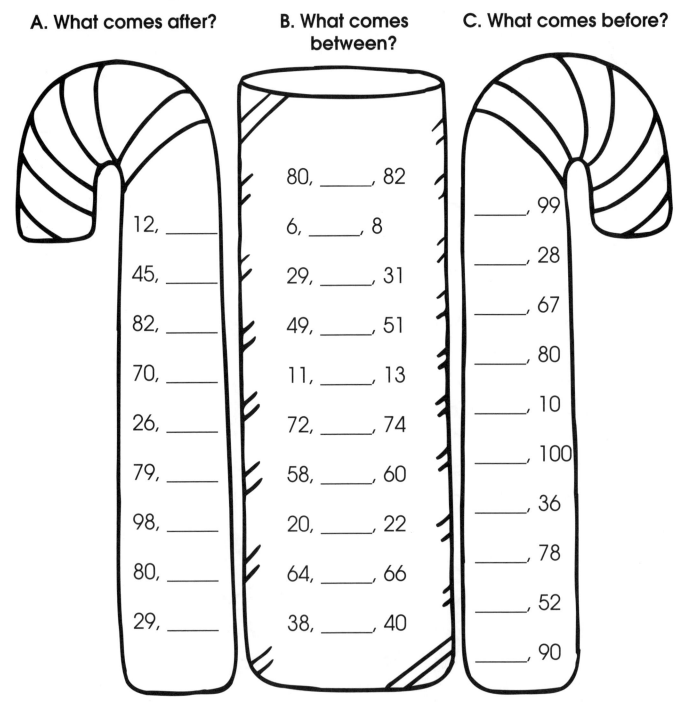

A. What comes after?

12, _____

45, _____

82, _____

70, _____

26, _____

79, _____

98, _____

80, _____

29, _____

B. What comes between?

80, _____, 82

6, _____, 8

29, _____, 31

49, _____, 51

11, _____, 13

72, _____, 74

58, _____, 60

20, _____, 22

64, _____, 66

38, _____, 40

C. What comes before?

_____, 99

_____, 28

_____, 67

_____, 80

_____, 10

_____, 100

_____, 36

_____, 78

_____, 52

_____, 90

Name

Greater than/less than   Unit 1

Greater means bigger or more. **Less** means smaller or fewer.

Circle the greater number of bugs in each row. Put an **X** on the least number of bugs in each row.

A.

B.

C.

D.

Draw bugs so the boxes are in order from least to greatest.

Less than		Greater than

Name

Comparing sets using <, >   Unit 1
There is a short way to write greater than and less than using signs. Their signs look like this:

> greater than   9 > 5   < less than   3 < 8

Compare the number of spots on each set of ladybugs.
Write > or < in the circle between them.

Name

Counting by 5s to 100   Unit 1

One way to count to 100 is counting by 5s. Practice counting by 5s using the number line.

← 5 10 15 20 25 30 35 40 45 50 55 60 65 70 75 80 85 90 95 100 →

Count by 5s to 100. Write the numbers on the hands. Use the fingers to help you.

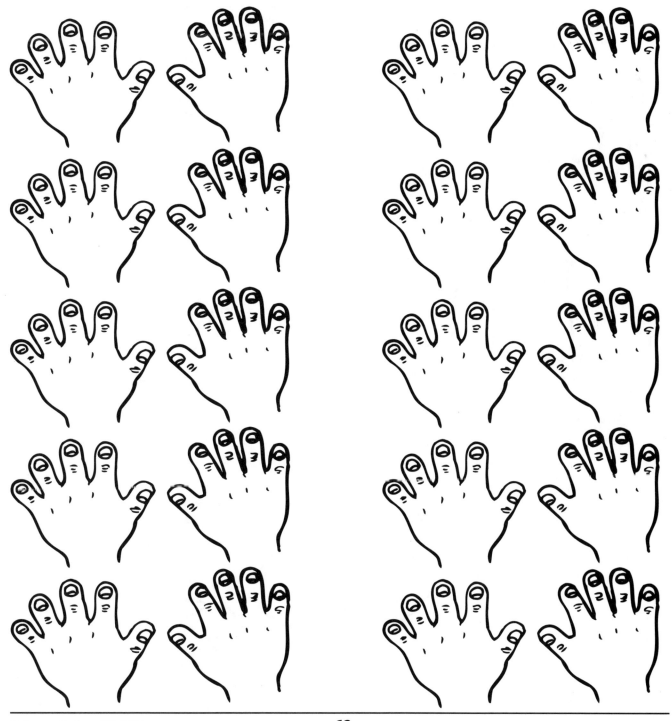

Name

Counting by 10s to 100

You can also count to 100 using 10s. Practice counting to 100 by 10s using the number line.

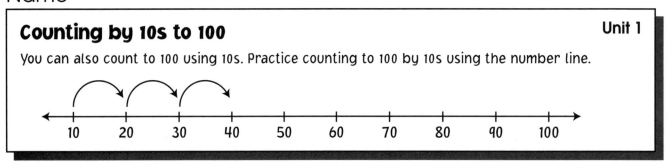

Count by 10s to connect each group of dots.

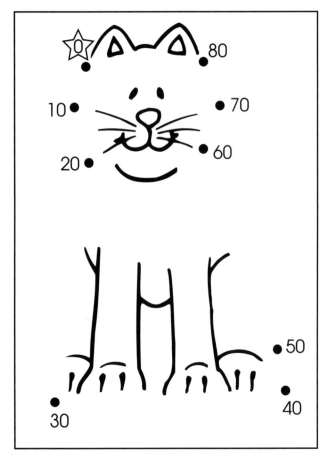

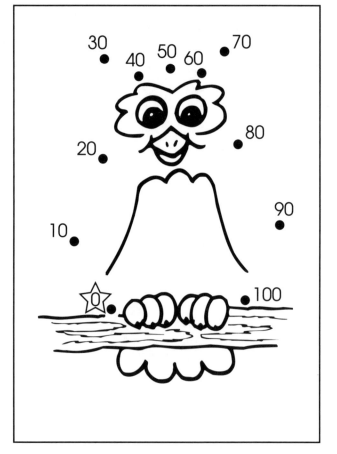

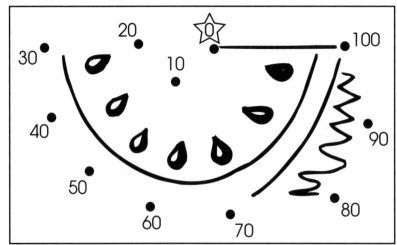

Name

Read or listen to the question. Fill in the circle beside the best answer.

❑ Example:

Which group shows the greatest number of balls?

(A) ○○○○○○ ○○○○○

(B) ○ ○ ○ ○ / ○ ○ ○ ○ / ○ ○ ○ ○

(C) ○ ○ ○ / ○ ○ ○ / ○ ○ ○

(D) ○ ○ ○ / ○ ○ ○ ○ ○

Always read or listen to each question carefully.

Answer: B because it is the group with the most balls.

Now try these. You have 20 minutes. Continue until you see .

---

1. How many petals are on the flower?

11   5   6   7
(A)   (B)   (C)   (D)

---

2. Which tree **does not** have a total of 7 apples?

(A)   (B)   (C)   (D)

 GO ON ▷

3. Which shelf has the most books?

 Ⓐ    Ⓑ    Ⓒ    Ⓓ

4. Which bus is **5th** from the school?

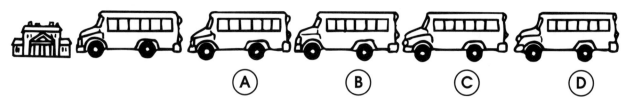

Ⓐ   Ⓑ   Ⓒ   Ⓓ

5. Which numbers are missing?   76, 77, 78, _____, _____, 81

| 80, 81 | 81, 82 | 82, 83 | 79, 80 |
| Ⓐ | Ⓑ | Ⓒ | Ⓓ |

6. What page number is next?

Ⓐ 81   Ⓑ 82

Ⓒ 84   Ⓓ 85

7. Which group is the **greatest**?

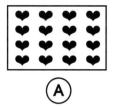 Ⓐ   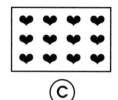 Ⓑ   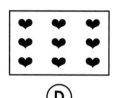 Ⓒ   Ⓓ

8. Which sign is missing?

18 ◯ 13

Ⓐ =   Ⓑ <

Ⓒ >   Ⓓ v

GO ON ▷

Unit 1 Test

9. This pattern shows counting by **5s**. What number is missing?

15, 20, _____, 30

(A) 25   (B) 40

(C) 21   (D) 23

10. Which number would you not say when counting by **10s**?

30
(A)

10
(B)

40
(C)

22
(D)

11. Which is the correct counting order?

(A) 19, 20, 18, 17   (B) 20, 17, 18, 19

(C) 17, 18, 19, 20   (D) 18, 20, 17, 19

12. What numbers are missing?   47, 48, _____, _____, 51

52, 53
(A)

49, 50
(B)

50, 52
(C)

59, 58
(D)

13. Which picture shows a sequence from largest to smallest?

(A)

(B)

(C)

(D)

GO ON

14. What place is the ♡ from the 🌀 ?

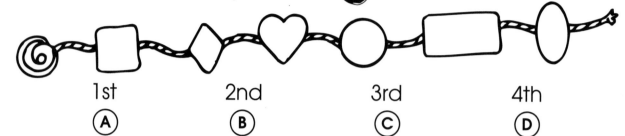

1st
(A)

2nd
(B)

3rd
(C)

4th
(D)

15. Which shows the correct counting order?

(A) 59, 60, 62, 61

(B) 62, 59, 60, 61

(C) 61, 62, 59, 60

(D) 59, 60, 61, 62

16. What number is missing?

89, _____, 91

90
(A)

92
(B)

88
(C)

87
(D)

17. Which group shows the **least**?

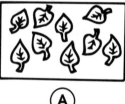
(A)

(B)

(C)

(D)

18. Which sign is missing?

6 9

(A) =

(B) <

(C) >

(D) –

GO ON

Name

Unit 1 Test

19. Which shows counting by **5s**?

    (A) 50, 55, 60, 65   (B) 50, 60, 70, 80

    (C) 50, 51, 52, 53   (D) 52, 54, 56, 58

20. Which shows counting by **10s**?

  60, 65, 70   80, 90, 100   80, 85, 90   80, 81, 82

    (A)   (B)   (C)   (D)

Write four numbers that show a pattern. What is the pattern?

Name

Groups of 10

Unit 2

Write the numbers 1–10. What makes 10 different from the other numbers? The number 10 is a two-digit number. It is written like this:

Tens	Ones
1	0

To count large groups, it is easiest to make groups of 10. The number of groups is written in the tens place. The number of leftover pieces is written in the ones place. Here's how it looks:

Tens	Ones
1	4

1 group of 10   4 leftovers

Circle each group of 10. Then write the number.

A.

Tens	Ones

B.

Tens	Ones

C.

Tens	Ones

D.

Tens	Ones

E.

Tens	Ones

F.

Tens	Ones

G.

Tens	Ones

H.

Tens	Ones

Place value with 2-digit numbers

Unit 2

Imagine taking ten small blocks and gluing them together like this:

□ □ □ □ □ □ □ □ □ □ = ⬚⬚⬚⬚⬚⬚⬚⬚⬚⬚

The block is now called a **ten**. The leftover blocks are called **ones**.

Count the tens and ones.

Name

There are four ways to show the same number.
Example:

 =

Tens	Ones
3	5

= 3 tens 5 ones = 35

Count the blocks and write each number three ways.

A. 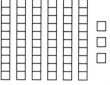 =

T	O

= _____ tens _____ ones = ☐

B. =

T	O

= _____ tens _____ ones = ☐

C. 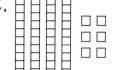 =

T	O

= _____ tens _____ ones = ☐

D. 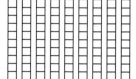 =

T	O

= _____ tens _____ ones = ☐

E. 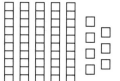 =

T	O

= _____ tens _____ ones = ☐

F 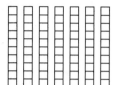 =

T	O

= _____ tens _____ ones = ☐

G. 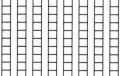  =

T	O

= _____ tens _____ ones = ☐

Name

Illustrating 2-digit numbers

There are four ways to show the same number.
Example:

72 = 7 tens 2 ones =

Tens	Ones
7	2

=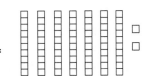

Write each number two ways. Then draw tens and ones blocks.

A.

83 = _____ tens _____ ones =

T	O

=

B.

65 = _____ tens _____ ones =

T	O

=

C.

40 = _____ tens _____ ones =

T	O

=

D.

23 = _____ tens _____ ones =

T	O

=

E.

28 = _____ tens _____ ones =

T	O

=

F.

37 = _____ tens _____ ones =

T	O

=

Name

Recording 3-digit numbers

Imagine taking 10 tens and gluing them together like this:

The block is now called a **hundred**.
The ten sticks are still tens, and
the leftover blocks are still **ones**. hundred ten □ one

Count and record the hundreds, tens, and ones.

A.    =

H	T	O

=

B. 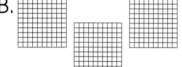 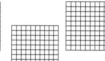   =

H	T	O

=

C. 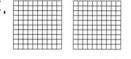 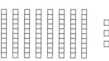 =

H	T	O

=

D. 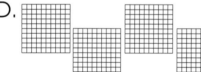 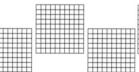 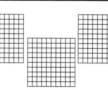 =

H	T	O

=

E. 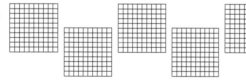   =

H	T	O

=

F. 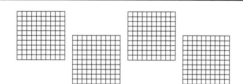 =

H	T	O

=

G.  =

H	T	O

=

Name

Place value with 3-digit numbers   Unit 2

When you see a 3-digit number, remember that you are looking at a hundreds place, tens place, and ones place.

Write each number another way.

Then draw hundreds blocks ,

tens blocks ⫿ , and ones blocks ☐.

A.
_____ hundreds

402 = _____ tens   =

_____ ones

B.
_____ hundreds

523 = _____ tens   =

_____ ones

C.
_____ hundreds

630 = _____ tens   =

_____ ones

D.
_____ hundreds

241 = _____ tens   =

_____ ones

 Choose a 3-digit number. Show the number three ways.

Name

numbers have names that can be written as words. Examples:

two = 2   five = 5   eight = 8   eleven = 11   fourteen = 14   nineteen = 19

Use the clues to complete the puzzle. The number words in the Word Bank will help you.

Across

1. 16
4. 17
9. 20
10. 11
11. 10

Down

2. 12
3. 14
5. 18
6. 13
7. 19
8. 15

Word Bank

ten
eleven
twelve
thirteen
fourteen
fifteen
sixteen
seventeen
eighteen
nineteen
twenty

Name _____

Recognizing numbers to 99 in word form   Unit 2

Names of numbers with a tens name and a ones name use a hyphen (-) in-between.
Example: forty-four

Which ant will reach the picnic basket first? Starting with column A, write the number words and color the matching square as you go. The first ant to reach the basket is the winner!

13   21   75   91   86   45

A.

eighty-six = _____

ninety-one = _____

forty-five = _____

sixty-two = _____

seventy-four = _____

seventy-five = _____

twenty-one = _____

thirteen = _____

thirty = _____

B.

forty-nine = _____

fifty-six = _____

fifty-eight = _____

ninety = _____

nineteen = _____

eighty-four = _____

eighty-five = _____

sixty-seven = _____

seventy-six = _____

58   19   84   67   76

62   74   30   49   56

10   68   85   90

Name

Using ‹ and › to compare 2-digit numbers   Unit 2

To compare 2-digit numbers, follow these steps:

1. Look at the tens place. The bigger number is greater.   7̲2 › 3̲9
2. If the tens are the same, look at the ones place.   3̲4 ‹ 3̲8

Remember: ‹ = less than   › = greater than

Write < or > to compare the numbers.

A. 19 ( ) 31

B. 23 ( ) 17

C. 40 ( ) 20

D. 78 ( ) 90

E. 84 ( ) 49

F. 38 ( ) 32

G. 76 ( ) 77

H. 73 ( ) 37

I. 57 ( ) 66

J. 61 ( ) 67

Name

Using clues to find numbers   Unit 2

Read the clues on each magnifying glass.
Find the number that
matches the clue in
the Number Bank.
Write the number
on the blank.

57	30	8	76
46	27	92	15

A. I will find thirteen plus two.

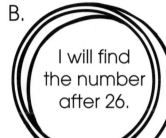

B. I will find the number after 26.

C. I will find a number greater than 89.

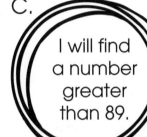

D. I will find the number after 20 when you count by tens.

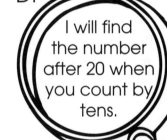

E. I will find forty-three plus three.

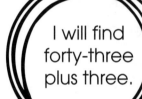

F. I will find a number less than ten.

G. I will find a number between 50 and 59.

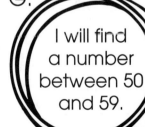

H. I will find a number between 75 and 80.

Name

Unit 2 Test

numeration Part II

Read or listen to the question. Fill in the circle beside the best answer.

❑ Example:
Which number has a 9 in the tens place?

189   693   209   904
Ⓐ   Ⓑ   Ⓒ   Ⓓ

Read all of the choices before you answer.

Answer: B

Now try these. You have 20 minutes. Continue until you see ⬡STOP.

---

1. Which matches the picture?

- Ⓐ 1 ten 3 ones
- Ⓑ 3 tens 1 one
- Ⓒ 1 ten 1 ones
- Ⓓ 3 tens 3 ones

---

2. How many blocks are there?

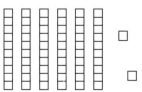

Ⓐ 60   Ⓑ 36

Ⓒ 63   Ⓓ 90

---

3. Which number has a 7 in the ones place?

471   704   670   417
Ⓐ   Ⓑ   Ⓒ   Ⓓ

---

4. How many tens and ones are in 84?

8 tens	8 tens	4 tens	84 tens
8 ones	4 ones	8 ones	0 ones
Ⓐ	Ⓑ	Ⓒ	Ⓓ

GO ON ▷

Unit 2 Test

5. How many marbles are there?

    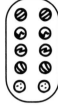

(A) 235   (B) 200

(C) 205   (D) 203

6. Which **does not** show **241**?

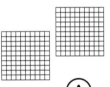

H	T	O
2	4	1

H	T	O
4	2	1

2 hundreds
4 tens
1 one

(A)   (B)   (C)   (D)

7. Which number is **fifty-three**?

35   53   503   350

(A)   (B)   (C)   (D)

8. Mark the number word for **19**.

nineteen   ninety   eleven   one

(A)   (B)   (C)   (D)

9. Which number sentence is true?

19 > 73   23 > 47   87 < 15   61 < 92

(A)   (B)   (C)   (D)

10. I am < seventy-five. Who am I?

79   92   83   61

(A)   (B)   (C)   (D)

GO ON

Unit 2 Test

11. Which shows

T	O
1	5	?

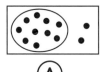
Ⓐ

Ⓑ

Ⓒ

Ⓓ

12. Mark the picture with 38 blocks.

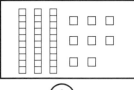
Ⓐ

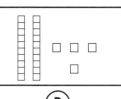
Ⓑ

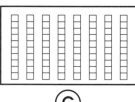
Ⓒ

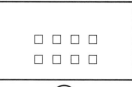
Ⓓ

13. Which **does not** equal **62**?

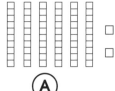
Ⓐ

T	O
6	2
Ⓑ

Ⓒ

6 tens
2 ones
Ⓓ

14. Mark the number with 4 tens and 6 ones.

64   106   46   406
Ⓐ   Ⓑ   Ⓒ   Ⓓ

15. Which number has a 6 in the hundreds place?

261   376   406   619
Ⓐ   Ⓑ   Ⓒ   Ⓓ

16. Find the **greatest** number.

T	O
7	2
Ⓐ

ninety-eight
Ⓑ

6 tens
3 ones
Ⓒ

Ⓓ

GO ON

Unit 2 Test

17. Which picture shows **307**?

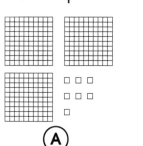 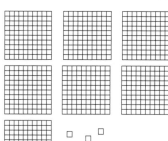

(A)　　　　(B)　　　　(C)　　　　(D)

18. Mark the number word that matches the sign.

(A) thirteen　　(B) thirty

(C) thirty-three　　(D) three

19. What page is the picture on?

(A) seventy-nine

(B) seventy-eight

(C) eighty

(D) sixty-eight

20. What will make the number sentence true?　58 ◯ 72

=
 (A)　　　>
 (B)　　　<
 (C)　　　v
 (D)

Write a 3-digit number with 6 in the tens place. How do you know the 6 is in the tens place?

STOP

Name

Shapes

Shapes are named by the number of sides they have. You may recognize these:

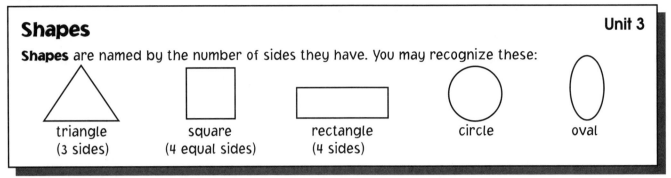

triangle
(3 sides)

square
(4 equal sides)

rectangle
(4 sides)

circle

oval

Use the picture of hidden shapes to complete
the garden notebook page.

Name

Shapes that are drawn on paper are flat, but shapes in our world are usually not.

Use the clues to find the object that each child "spies."

I spy a
Color it red.

I spy a
Color it blue.

I spy a
Color it yellow.

I spy a
Color it orange.

I spy a
Color it green.

I spy a
Color it purple.

CANDY

35

Identifying shapes   Unit 3

Uh oh! The lunches in Ms. Nook's class have gotten mixed up.
Use the clues to match each lunchbox with its owner.

Name

Lines of symmetry

Imagine folding a shape in half so that both sides are exactly the same. The fold line is called a **line of symmetry** and it looks like this: not this:

Draw a line to show two parts that are exactly alike.

Draw the other half of each food so that the sides are exactly alike.

Think of another food that has a line of symmetry. Draw it. Add the line of symmetry.

Name

Congruent shapes

Some shapes are exactly the same size and shape. It is like having a twin!

Color the shape that is exactly the same size and shape as the first.

A.

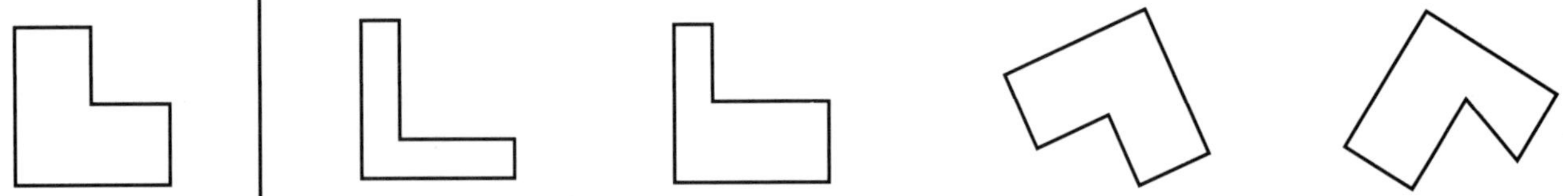

B.

C.

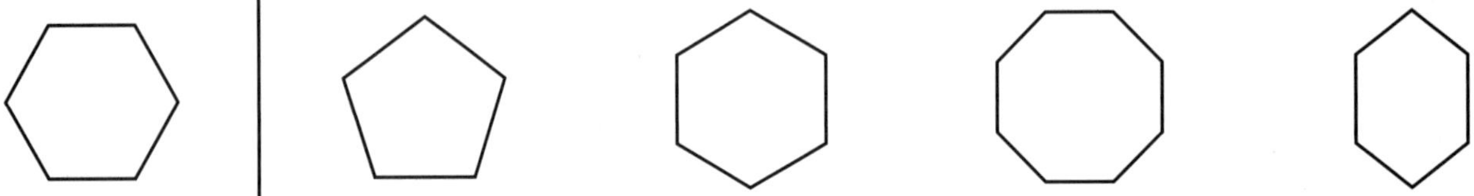

D.

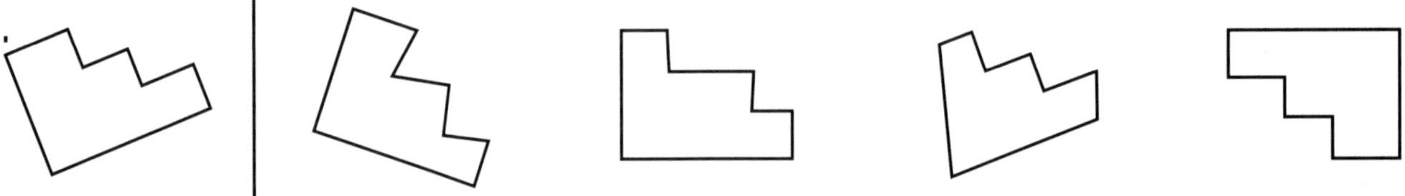

E.

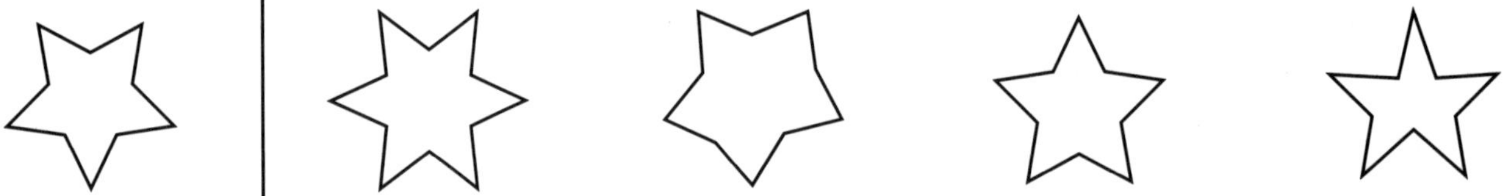

F.

G.

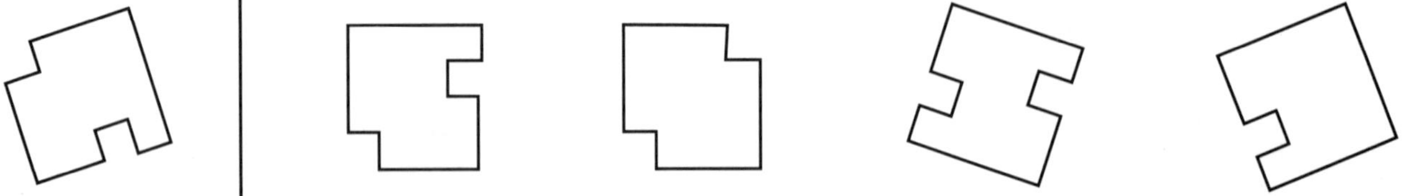

H.

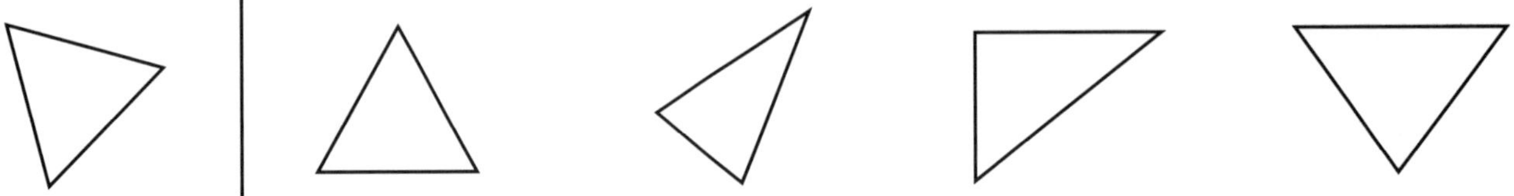

38

Name

Similar shapes

Some shapes look alike, but one is bigger than the other. It is like looking at a mother and its baby!

Circle the picture that is the same shape, but a different size.

A.

B.

C.

D.

E.

F.

G.

H.

Name

Patterns

Patterns are repeating pictures or numbers that can be predicted.

Continue each pattern by drawing pictures.

A.

B.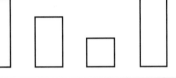

C.

D.

E.

F.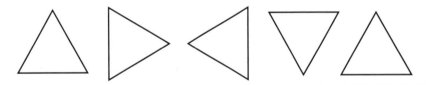

G.

H.

Name

Sequencing

Unit 3

A **sequence** is the order that something happens.

Label **1**, **2**, **3**, and **4** to show which happens 1st, 2nd, 3rd, and 4th.

A. B. C. D. E.

Teach & Test Math: Grade 1

Name

Read or listen to the question. Fill in the circle beside the best answer.

❏ Example:
Which group of lines could be used to make a rectangle?

(A) 　(B)

(C) 　(D)

With picture answers, cover some of the choices so you see only one picture at a time.

Answer: A because it takes 2 short lines and 2 long lines to make a rectangle.

Now try these. You have 20 minutes. Continue until you see .

---

1. Which is most like the shape of the box?　

(A) ◯　(B) ▭

(C) △　(D) ⬭

---

2. How many sides does a square have?

none　　　1　　　3　　　4
(A)　　　(B)　　　(C)　　　(D)

---

3. Which group could be used to make a triangle?

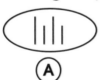　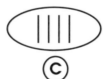　◯ⅠⅠⅠⅠ　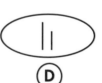

(A)　　　(B)　　　(C)　　　(D)

GO ON ▷

4. Which group shows the fewest circles?

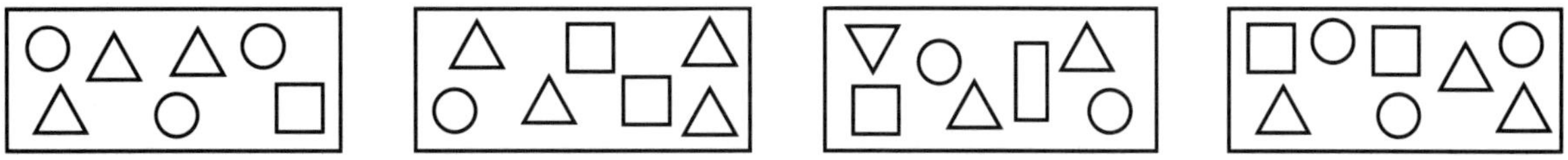

Ⓐ   Ⓑ   Ⓒ   Ⓓ

5. Which shows a circle in a rectangle?

Ⓐ   Ⓑ   Ⓒ   Ⓓ

6. Which shape shows a fold line that makes both sides the same?

Ⓐ   Ⓑ   Ⓒ   Ⓓ

7. Which shape is exactly like the first?

Ⓐ   Ⓑ   Ⓒ   Ⓓ

8. Which picture shows the same shape, but smaller?

Ⓐ   Ⓑ   Ⓒ   Ⓓ

GO ON ▷

9. What comes next?

   (A)   (B)   (C)   (D)

10. Finish the pattern.

     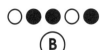      

   (A)   (B)   (C)   (D)

11. Which object is most like the shape in the box?

            (A)   (B)   (C)   (D)

12. How many sides does this shape have?

    2   3   4   5

    (A)   (B)   (C)   (D)

13. Mark the picture that shows the inside the .

   (A)   (B)   (C)   (D)

GO ON

Name

Use the picture for questions 14 and 15.

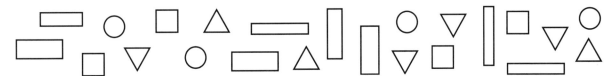

14. How many triangles are in the picture?

5
Ⓐ

6
Ⓑ

7
Ⓒ

8
Ⓓ

15. How many shapes in the picture have four sides?

10
Ⓐ

12
Ⓑ

14
Ⓒ

16
Ⓓ

16. If this shape was folded on the line, which would be the missing half?

Ⓐ

Ⓑ

Ⓒ

Ⓒ

Ⓓ

17. Which group shows two shapes that are not alike?

Ⓐ

Ⓑ

Ⓒ

Ⓓ

GO ON

18. Which of these is not the same shape?

(A)   (B)   (C)   (D)

19. Which shows the correct order?

(A)   (B)   (C)   (D)

20. Finish the pattern:

(A)   (B)   (C)   (D)

How are these two shapes the same? How are they different?

STOP

Name

Adding means putting groups together. The symbol for adding is called a plus sign (+).
Example: 3 + 5

Use the jewels on the jeans to help you add.

A.

4 + 2 = _____

B.

5 + 4 = _____

C.

4 + 6 = _____

D.

3 + 3 = _____

E.

9 + 0 = _____

F.

2 + 8 = _____

G.

9 + 1 = _____

H.

5 + 5 = _____

I.

5 + 3 = _____

J.

3 + 6 = _____

K.

4 + 3 = _____

Draw jewels
and write
your own
number
sentence.

Name

This is how an addition problem is written: 4 + 3 = 7. This is also called a number sentence. The answer is called the sum (7).

Use the beads to write addition problems.

A.
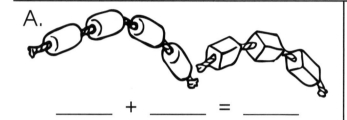
_____ + _____ = _____

B.
_____ + _____ = _____

C.
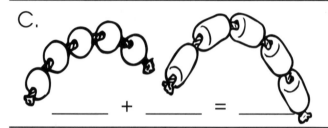
_____ + _____ = _____

D.
_____ + _____ = _____

E.
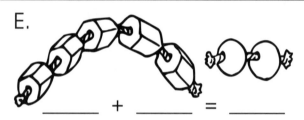
_____ + _____ = _____

F.
_____ + _____ = _____

G.
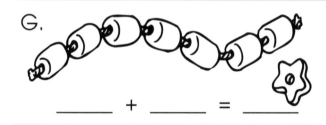
_____ + _____ = _____

H.
_____ + _____ = _____

I.
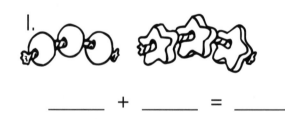
_____ + _____ = _____

J.
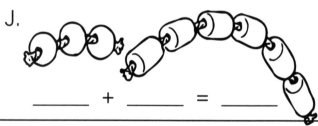
_____ + _____ = _____

K.
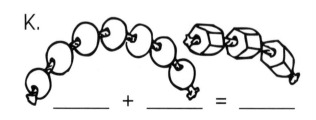
_____ + _____ = _____

L.
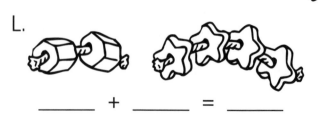
_____ + _____ = _____

Finding sums to 18

You can add numbers without pictures or a number line. Here's how:
Keep the larger number in your head. Count on using your fingers.

Find the sums. Then use the code to answer the riddle.

Where do freshwater fish keep their money?

In a ___ ___ ___ ___ ___
17   12   15   11   17

___ ___ ___ ___ !
14   16   13   18

	E		I
$3 + 8 =$ ___		$6 + 6 =$ ___	
	C		N
$6 + 3 =$ ___		$7 + 6 =$ ___	
	R		L
$8 + 9 =$ ___		$5 + 5 =$ ___	
	P		B
$4 + 4 =$ ___		$7 + 7 =$ ___	
	A		V
$8 + 8 =$ ___		$7 + 8 =$ ___	
	S		K
$3 + 4 =$ ___		$9 + 9 =$ ___	

Finding the sum of 3 addends

Unit 4

You can add three numbers together! Find a hidden problem that you already know, add the numbers, then add the third number. Example:

7 + 3 + 5 = 15   (Add 7 + 3 = 10, 10 + 5 = 15.)

Find the sums.

A. 6 + 4 + 2 =

B. 5 + 4 + 6 =

C. 4 + 3 + 7 =

D. 6 + 2 + 8 =

E. 9 + 4 + 3 =

F. 5 + 4 + 9 =

G. 7 + 2 + 5 =

H. 6 + 2 + 6 =

I. 3 + 2 + 4 =

J. 1 + 1 + 1 =

K. 7 + 3 + 2 =

L. 4 + 4 + 8 =

M. 2 + 2 + 4 =

N. 3 + 4 + 3 =

O. 2 + 8 + 7 =

P. 3 + 3 + 7 =

Q. 4 + 3 + 8 =

R. 3 + 3 + 3 =

Finding the sum of 3 addends

Use the code to find the sum of each word.

A	B	C	D	E	F	G	H	I	J	K	L	M
5	4	1	2	5	4	4	4	5	4	6	2	7

N	O	P	Q	R	S	T	U	V	W	X	Y	Z
9	5	3	6	5	3	4	5	6	8	4	2	1

A. map

_____ + _____ + _____ = _____

B. jar

_____ + _____ + _____ = _____

C. few

_____ + _____ + _____ = _____

D. net

_____ + _____ + _____ = _____

E. him

_____ + _____ + _____ = _____

F. big

_____ + _____ + _____ = _____

G. top

_____ + _____ + _____ = _____

H. for

_____ + _____ + _____ = _____

I. mud

_____ + _____ + _____ = _____

J. cup

_____ + _____ + _____ = _____

K. saw

_____ + _____ + _____ = _____

L. wax

_____ + _____ + _____ = _____

Name

Adding 2-digit numbers (no regrouping)   Unit 4

To add 2-digit numbers, follow these steps:

1. Add the ones.

T	O
2	7
+ 3	1
	8

2. Add the tens.

T	O
2	7
+ 3	1
5	8

Help Aunt Rosie decide which hat to wear. Answer each problem and color its sum on the hats as you go. The first hat to be completely colored is the hat Aunt Rosie will wear.

35	42	63	17	76	42
+ 34	+ 51	+ 24	+ 32	+ 12	+ 30

32	61	33	25	30	24
+ 21	+ 30	+ 31	+ 13	+ 40	+ 32

35	23	32	61	50
+ 2	+ 22	+ 35	+ 31	+ 30

91	87	93
38	72	53
45	67	60

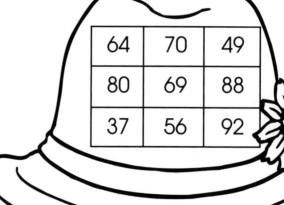

64	70	49
80	69	88
37	56	92

Name

Adding 3-digit numbers (no regrouping)
Unit 4

To add 3-digit numbers, follow these steps:

1. Add the ones.

H	T	O
	3	1	4
+	1	0	3
			7

2. Add the tens.

H	T	O
	3	1	4
+	1	0	3
		1	7

3. Add the hundreds.

H	T	O
	3	1	4
+	1	0	3
	4	1	7

Find the sums.

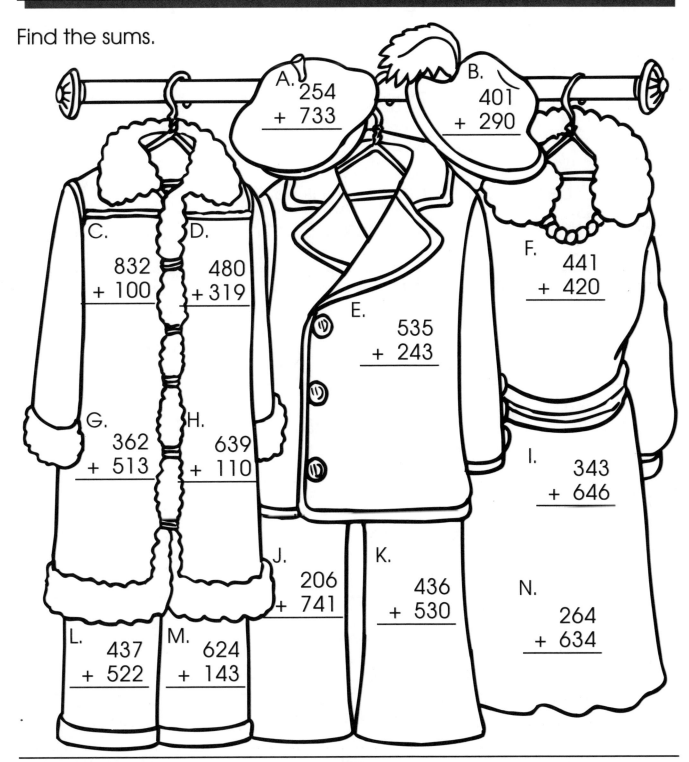

A. 254 + 733

B. 401 + 290

C. 832 + 100

D. 480 + 319

E. 535 + 243

F. 441 + 420

G. 362 + 513

H. 639 + 110

I. 343 + 646

J. 206 + 741

K. 436 + 530

L. 437 + 522

M. 624 + 143

N. 264 + 634

Name

Addition Computation

Read or listen to the question. Use an extra piece of paper to work on the problems. Fill in the circle beside the best answer.

❑ Example:
Find the sum.

$$\begin{array}{r} 31 \\ + 14 \\ \hline \end{array}$$

Ⓐ 38   Ⓑ 52
Ⓒ 75   Ⓓ 45

Find your own answer before reading the choices.

Answer: D because the correct sum is 45.

Now try these. You have 20 minutes. Continue until you see .

---

1. Which does not equal 12?

| 6 + 6 | 7 + 5 | 9 + 4 | 2 + 10 |
| Ⓐ | Ⓑ | Ⓒ | Ⓓ |

---

2. $$\begin{array}{r} 231 \\ + 304 \\ \hline \end{array}$$

| 607 | 535 | 565 | 505 |
| Ⓐ | Ⓑ | Ⓒ | Ⓓ |

---

3. Which is correct?

| 5 + 5 = 9 | 5 + 5 = 10 | 5 + 5 = 11 | 5 + 5 = 12 |
| Ⓐ | Ⓑ | Ⓒ | Ⓓ |

---

4. $$\begin{array}{r} 62 \\ + 14 \\ \hline \end{array}$$

| 76 | 67 | 85 | 69 |
| Ⓐ | Ⓑ | Ⓒ | Ⓓ |

GO ON ⟩

Name

5. Which number sentence matches the picture?

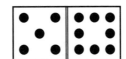

- (A) $5 + 8 = 13$
- (B) $6 + 7 = 13$
- (C) $5 + 5 = 10$
- (D) $5 + 7 = 12$

6. $7 + 8 =$

13	15	16	14
(A)	(B)	(C)	(D)

7. Which fact is not true?

$5 + 6 = 11$	$3 + 5 = 8$	$7 + 6 = 13$	$6 + 6 = 14$
(A)	(B)	(C)	(D)

8. Which number sentence matches $9 + 5$?

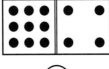   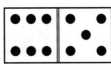   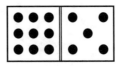   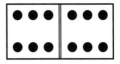

(A)   (B)   (C)   (D)

9. $8 + 3 =$

11	12	13	14
(A)	(B)	(C)	(D)

10. $6 + 4 + 3 =$

12	13	14	15
(A)	(B)	(C)	(D)

GO ON

Unit 4 Test

11. Fill in the missing number.

$7 + \underline{\quad} = 14$

6   7   8   9
Ⓐ   Ⓑ   Ⓒ   Ⓓ

12. Find the sum.

$\begin{array}{r} 51 \\ + 47 \\ \hline \end{array}$

67   92   97   98
Ⓐ   Ⓑ   Ⓒ   Ⓓ

13. Which problem matches the picture?

Ⓐ 6 + 4

Ⓑ 5 + 5

Ⓒ 6 + 6

Ⓓ 6 + 5

14.

$\begin{array}{r} 304 \\ + 284 \\ \hline \end{array}$

804   580   588   508
Ⓐ   Ⓑ   Ⓒ   Ⓓ

15. Which is not true?

$4 + 3 = 7$ $8 + 7 = 15$ $6 + 6 = 12$ $4 + 8 = 11$
Ⓐ   Ⓑ   Ⓒ   Ⓓ

GO ON

Unit 4 Test

16.

$$\begin{array}{r} 8 \\ + 8 \\ \hline \end{array}$$

14 Ⓐ   16 Ⓑ   12 Ⓒ   18 Ⓓ

17.

$9 + \boxed{} = 18$

7 Ⓐ   8 Ⓑ   9 Ⓒ   11 Ⓓ

18.

$7 + 3 = \boxed{}$

10 Ⓐ   11 Ⓑ   12 Ⓒ   13 Ⓓ

19.

$$\begin{array}{r} 432 \\ + 167 \\ \hline \end{array}$$

598 Ⓐ   905 Ⓑ   699 Ⓒ   599 Ⓓ

20.

$9 + \boxed{} = 16$

7 Ⓐ   8 Ⓑ   9 Ⓒ   11 Ⓓ

Write a number sentence. Draw a picture to tell about it.

STOP

Midway Review Test

Read or listen to the question. Use an extra piece of paper to work on problems. Fill in the circle beside the best answer.

Remember your Helping Hand Strategies:

 1. Always read or listen to each question carefully.

❑ Example:
Find the sum.

$$\begin{array}{r} 26 \\ + 43 \\ \hline \end{array}$$

(A) 96
(B) 63
(C) 69
(D) 68

 2. Read all of the choices before you answer.

3. With picture answers, cover some of the choices so you see only one picture at a time.

Answer: C because the ones column equals 9, and the tens column equals 6.

Now try these. You have 25 minutes.

Continue until you see ⬡STOP.

 4. Find your own answer before reading the choices.

---

1. How many blocks are there?

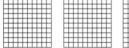

(A) 245   (B) 415

(C) 425   (D) 420

---

2. Which group shows the **fewest** squares?

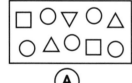  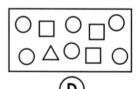

(A)   (B)   (C)   (D)

---

3. Which problem **is not** missing 9?

$9 + \boxed{} = 18$ $3 + \boxed{} = 12$ $5 + 4 = \boxed{}$ $7 + \boxed{} = 14$

(A)   (B)   (C)   (D)

GO ON ⟩

Name _____

4. Mark the numbers that are missing.

56, 57, 58, _____, _____, 61

60, 62	59, 60	59, 70	62, 63
(A)	(B)	(C)	(D)

5. Which **does not** equal 309?

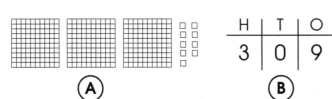

(A)	(B)	(C)	(D)

H | T | O
3 | 0 | 9

9 hundreds
3 tens
0 ones

3 hundreds
0 tens
9 ones

6. Which shape shows a folded line that makes both sides the same?

(A)	(B)	(C)	(D)

7.
```
  362
+ 421
```

837	783	641	743
(A)	(B)	(C)	(D)

8. Which number has an 8 in the ones place?

384	208	819	683
(A)	(B)	(C)	(D)

9. Which shows counting by **5s**?

(A) 30, 35, 40, 45   (B) 30, 31, 32, 33

(C) 30, 40, 50, 60   (D) 30, 40, 35, 45

GO ON ⟩

Midway Review Test

10. Finish the pattern.

    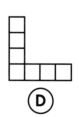

Ⓐ Ⓑ Ⓒ Ⓓ

11. Which number sentence matches the picture?

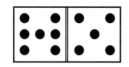

Ⓐ 6 + 5 = 11   Ⓑ 5 + 5 = 10

Ⓒ 7 + 5 = 12   Ⓓ 4 + 5 = 9

12. Mark the group with the most stars.

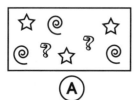 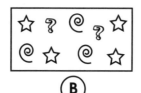  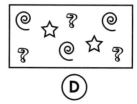

Ⓐ Ⓑ Ⓒ Ⓓ

13. What number word is missing? 10, 20, 30, _____, 50

thirty   forty   fifty   twenty
Ⓐ   Ⓑ   Ⓒ   Ⓓ

14. Which shape is exactly like the first?

   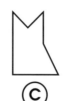

Ⓐ Ⓑ Ⓒ Ⓓ

15.
$$\begin{array}{r} 43 \\ + 52 \\ \hline \end{array}$$

95   75   59   94
Ⓐ   Ⓑ   Ⓒ   Ⓓ

GO ON

16. Which number sentence is true?

12 > 61   6 < 72   47 > 90   18 > 60
Ⓐ   Ⓑ   Ⓒ   Ⓓ

17. Mark the **greatest** number.

72   3 tens   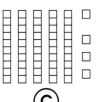 | T | O |
Ⓐ   5 ones | 8 | 1 |
            Ⓑ   Ⓒ   Ⓓ

18. Mark the picture with a triangle in a rectangle.

                    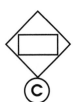   [shape D]
Ⓐ   Ⓑ   Ⓒ   Ⓓ

19.
$$\begin{array}{r} 654 \\ + 324 \\ \hline \end{array}$$

678   370   904   978
Ⓐ   Ⓑ   Ⓒ   Ⓓ

20. Which ball is 6th from the net?

                        Ⓐ   Ⓑ   Ⓒ   Ⓓ

Write a number sentence with a sum greater than 14. Show a way to solve the problem.

STOP

Name

Subtracting from 10 and less

Subtracting means taking away from a group. The symbol for subtracting is called a minus sign (–). Example: 9 – 4

To subtract, start with a large group and cross some out. The number that is left is your answer.

Use the pictures to help you subtract.

A. 8 – 3 = ☐

7 – 2 = ☐

10 – 4 = ☐

9 – 3 = ☐

B. 10 – 5 = ☐

8 – 4 = ☐

5 – 2 = ☐

7 – 3 = ☐

C. 6 – 3 = ☐

4 – 2 = ☐

9 – 5 = ☐

10 – 6 = ☐

D. 8 – 5 = ☐

6 – 4 = ☐

9 – 4 = ☐

10 – 4 = ☐

Writing a subtraction equation

Unit 5

This is how a subtraction problem is written. 8 – 4 = 4 The answer is called the difference (4).

Write a subtraction problem to match each picture. Then find the difference.

____ – ____ = ____   ____ – ____ = ____   ____ – ____ = ____

____ – ____ = ____   ____ – ____ = ____   ____ – ____ = ____

____ – ____ = ____   ____ – ____ = ____   ____ – ____ = ____

____ – ____ = ____   ____ – ____ = ____   ____ – ____ = ____

Subtracting from 14 and less

Some subtraction problems start with larger groups. You can find their differences the same way.

Cross out. Write the differences.

A.
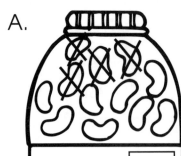
12 – 4 =

B.
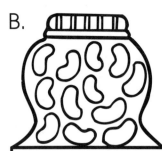
12 – 5 =

C.
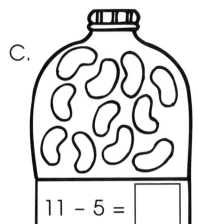
11 – 5 =

D.
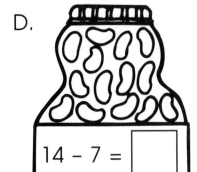
14 – 7 =

E.
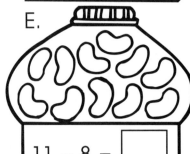
11 – 8 =

F.

13 – 5 =

G.
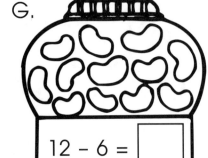
12 – 6 =

H.

14 – 8 =

I.

11 – 7 =

J.
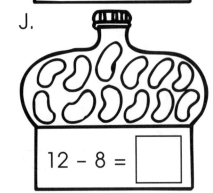
12 – 8 =

K.
14 – 5 =

L.
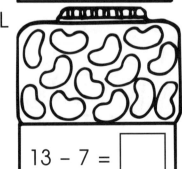
13 – 7 =

Subtracting from 14 and less

Another way to subtract is to use a number line. Start at the highest number and then count back. The number you land on is your answer.

Example:

$14 - 8 = 6$

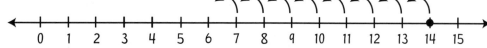

Use the number line to help you find the differences.

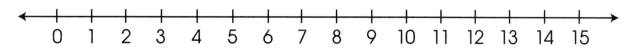

	A.	$\begin{array}{r} 11 \\ -\ 3 \\ \hline \end{array}$	$\begin{array}{r} 12 \\ -\ 6 \\ \hline \end{array}$	$\begin{array}{r} 13 \\ -\ 6 \\ \hline \end{array}$	$\begin{array}{r} 14 \\ -\ 9 \\ \hline \end{array}$
	B.	$\begin{array}{r} 11 \\ -\ 6 \\ \hline \end{array}$	$\begin{array}{r} 12 \\ -\ 4 \\ \hline \end{array}$	$\begin{array}{r} 13 \\ -\ 9 \\ \hline \end{array}$	$\begin{array}{r} 11 \\ -\ 4 \\ \hline \end{array}$
	C.	$\begin{array}{r} 12 \\ -\ 8 \\ \hline \end{array}$	$\begin{array}{r} 11 \\ -\ 7 \\ \hline \end{array}$	$\begin{array}{r} 13 \\ -\ 4 \\ \hline \end{array}$	$\begin{array}{r} 14 \\ -\ 7 \\ \hline \end{array}$
	D.	$\begin{array}{r} 12 \\ -\ 7 \\ \hline \end{array}$	$\begin{array}{r} 14 \\ -\ 8 \\ \hline \end{array}$	$\begin{array}{r} 11 \\ -\ 5 \\ \hline \end{array}$	$\begin{array}{r} 12 \\ -\ 5 \\ \hline \end{array}$
	E.	$\begin{array}{r} 11 \\ -\ 8 \\ \hline \end{array}$	$\begin{array}{r} 13 \\ -\ 7 \\ \hline \end{array}$	$\begin{array}{r} 14 \\ -\ 5 \\ \hline \end{array}$	$\begin{array}{r} 13 \\ -\ 8 \\ \hline \end{array}$

Name

Did you know that adding and subtracting are like cousins? The numbers used in an addition problem can be turned around and used to make subtraction problems. The three numbers used are related to each other, and they are called a **fact family**.

Example:
7   9   16

7 + 9 = 16	16 − 7 = 9
9 + 7 = 16	16 − 9 = 7

Write two addition and two subtraction problems for each fact family.

A.

7   5   12

____ + ____ = ____

____ + ____ = ____

____ − ____ = ____

____ − ____ = ____

B.

____ + ____ = ____

____ + ____ = ____

____ − ____ = ____

____ − ____ = ____

8

7

15

C.

____ + ____ = ____

____ + ____ = ____

____ − ____ = ____

____ − ____ = ____

9

8

17

D.

8   6   14

____ + ____ = ____

____ + ____ = ____

____ − ____ = ____

____ − ____ = ____

Name

Subtracting from 18 and less

You can use the number line to subtract larger numbers as well.

Example: 17 − 9 = 8

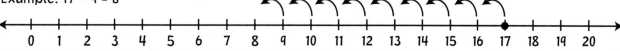

Find the differences.

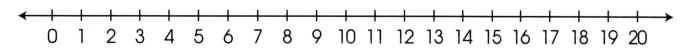

A.
$$15 - 8$$
$$16 - 7$$
$$18 - 9$$
$$14 - 9$$
$$17 - 9$$

B.
$$17 - 8$$
$$13 - 6$$
$$15 - 6$$
$$16 - 8$$
$$12 - 7$$

C.
$$16 - 9$$
$$14 - 8$$
$$12 - 6$$
$$15 - 7$$
$$12 - 5$$

D.
$$15 - 9$$
$$11 - 4$$
$$17 - 9$$

 Write three subtraction problems that have the same answer.

Name

Subtracting from 18 and less

Use what you know about fact families to find missing numbers.

Unit 5

Find the missing numbers. Then use the code to answer the riddle.

How are the earth and a loaf of bread alike?

___ ___ ___ ___   ___ ___ ___ ___
18   8   9   6   15   7   18   8

___ ___ ___ ___   ___
8   4   5   9   4

___ ___ ___ ___ ___!
16   14   11   17   18

$15 - 8 = \boxed{}$ **O**	$17 - 8 = \boxed{}$ **E**
$\boxed{} - 9 = 7$ **C**	$11 - 7 = \boxed{}$ **A**
$12 - 6 = \boxed{}$ **Y**	$\boxed{} - 9 = 9$ **T**
$\boxed{} - 9 = 8$ **S**	$\boxed{} - 7 = 7$ **R**
$16 - 8 = \boxed{}$ **H**	$\boxed{} - 5 = 6$ **U**
$12 - 7 = \boxed{}$ **V**	$\boxed{} - 8 = 7$ **B**

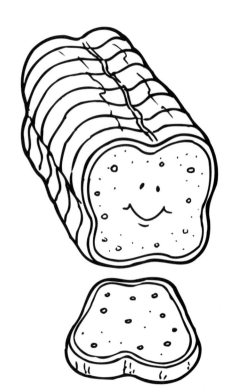

Name

Subtracting 2-digit numbers   Unit 5

To subtract from 2-digit numbers, follow these steps:

1. Subtract the ones.

T	O
8	9
− 4	2
	7

2. Subtract the tens.

T	O
8	9
− 4	2
4	7

Did you know that the sailfish is the fastest fish? It can swim up to 60 miles per hour. That is the speed limit on some highways! Find the differences to try to catch the fish.

A.
```
  79        98        94        76        91        76
- 56      - 45      - 52      - 10      - 40      - 31
```

B.
```
  57        26        75        84        72        87
- 13      - 14      - 23      - 41      - 60      - 34
```

C.
```
  38        47        67        78        49        77
- 27      -  5      - 33      - 52      - 16      - 25
```

Subtracting 3-digit numbers

Unit 5

To subtract from 3-digit numbers, follow these steps:

1. Subtract the ones.

	H	T	O
	7	3	5
−	2	0	3
			2

2. Subtract the tens.

	H	T	O
	7	3	5
−	2	0	3
		3	2

3. Subtract the hundreds.

	H	T	O
	7	3	5
−	2	0	3
	5	3	2

Find the differences. Then find the answer to the fun fact by writing the circled numbers in order.

A man in Australia once caught a shark on his fishing line! How much did it weigh?

It weighed _____, _____ _____ _____ **pounds!**

A.
$$374 - 152$$
$$685 - 353 \bigcirc$$
$$998 - 367$$
$$789 - 443 \bigcirc$$

B.
$$298 - 43$$
$$575 - 233$$
$$896 - 432$$
$$768 - 502 \bigcirc$$

C.
$$921 - 510 \bigcirc$$
$$762 - 141$$
$$306 - 102$$
$$919 - 603$$

Name

Unit 5 Test

Subtraction Computation

Page 1

Read or listen to the question. Use an extra piece of paper to write problems and work on them. Fill in the circle beside the best answer.

When using scratch paper, copy carefully.

❏ Example:
Find the difference.

$$\begin{array}{r} 76 \\ -\ 32 \\ \hline \end{array}$$

(A) 44   (B) 34

(C) 48   (D) 46

Answer: A because the ones column equals 4, and the tens column equals 4.

Now try these. You have 20 minutes. Continue until you see ⬡STOP.

---

1. Which **does not** equal 4?

| 7 – 3 | 10 – 6 | 8 – 5 | 8 – 4 |
| (A) | (B) | (C) | (D) |

---

2. Which number sentence matches the picture?

(A) 7 – 4 = 3

(B) 8 – 3 = 5

(C) 6 – 1 = 5

(D) 4 – 3 = 1

---

3. 14 – 7 =

| 3 | 5 | 4 | 7 |
| (A) | (B) | (C) | (D) |

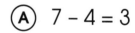
GO ON ➤

© Carson-Dellosa CD-4305

Teach & Test Math: Grade 1

4. Which problem matches this number line?

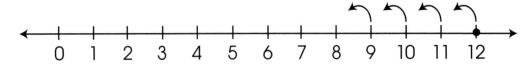

$8 - 4 = 4$
(A)

$12 - 4 = 8$
(B)

$12 - 9 = 3$
(C)

$12 - 8 = 4$
(D)

5. Which **does not** belong to the fact family?

$7 + 9 = 16$
(A)

$9 + 7 = 16$
(B)

$16 - 7 = 9$
(C)

$9 - 7 = 2$
(D)

6. $18 - 9 =$

7
(A)

8
(B)

9
(C)

6
(D)

7.
$$\begin{array}{r} 645 \\ - 203 \\ \hline \end{array}$$

442
(A)

402
(B)

848
(C)

448
(D)

8. Which number sentence **is not** missing 6?

$12 - \boxed{} = 6$
(A)

$10 - 4 = \boxed{}$
(B)

$9 - \boxed{} = 3$
(C)

$11 - 4 = \boxed{}$
(D)

9.
$$\begin{array}{r} 97 \\ - 45 \\ \hline \end{array}$$

25
(A)

52
(B)

62
(C)

42
(D)

GO ON

Name

10. 11 – 6 =

5 (A) 6 (B) 7 (C) 8 (D)

11. 9 – 6 =

4 (A) 5 (B) 3 (C) 2 (D)

12. Which problem matches the picture?

⊗ ⊗ ⊗ ○ ○ ○
⊗ ⊗ ○ ○ ○ ○

(A) 12 – 5 = 7
(B) 12 – 6 = 6
(C) 11 – 5 = 5
(D) 12 – 7 = 5

13. Which number sentence **does not** equal 5?

14 – 9 = ☐ (A)   16 – 9 = ☐ (B)   12 – 7 = ☐ (C)   13 – 8 = ☐ (D)

14. 13 – 6 =

5 (A) 6 (B) 7 (C) 8 (D)

15. Which number is missing from the fact family?

13 – ☐ = 5   ☐ + 5 = 13

5 + ☐ = 13   13 – 5 = ☐

(A) 7
(B) 8
(C) 9
(D) 6

GO ON

Unit 5 Test

16. $16 - 8 =$

    8 (A)   6 (B)   5 (C)   7 (D)

17. $14 - 5 =$

    6 (A)   7 (B)   8 (C)   9 (D)

18.

$10 - \boxed{} = 3$

    6 (A)   7 (B)   8 (C)   9 (D)

19.

$$\begin{array}{r} 87 \\ -\ 53 \\ \hline \end{array}$$

    34 (A)   45 (B)   57 (C)   36 (D)

20.

$$\begin{array}{r} 697 \\ -\ 81 \\ \hline \end{array}$$

    628 (A)   618 (B)   616 (C)   626 (D)

Write four number sentences using 17, 8, and 9. Why are these numbers called a fact family?

STOP

Name

Identifying and counting coins

Unit 6

Do you recognize these coins?

To count coins, follow these steps:

1. Group all of the pennies together, all of the nickels together, and all of the dimes together.
2. Count the dimes first. Count by 10s.
3. Count the nickels next. Count by 5s.
4. Count the pennies last. Count by 1s.

penny = 1¢

nickel = 5¢

dime = 10¢

Count the coins.

Teach & Test Math: Grade 1

Name

Identifying and counting coins

Have you seen this coin before?

Try these steps to count with more coins:

1. Group all of the like coins together.
2. Count the quarters.
3. Count the dimes.
4. Count the nickels.
5. Count the pennies.

quarter = 25¢

Count the coins.

Marking coins to equate given amounts

Unit 6

Which coins equal 23¢? To find them, ask yourself:

1. Can I use any quarters? (no)
2. Can I use any dimes? How many? (yes, 2 dimes = 20¢)
3. Can I use any nickels? How many? (no)
4. Can I use any pennies? How many? (yes, 3 pennies = 3¢)

Circle the coins needed to make the given amount.

A. 14¢

B. 21¢

C. 7¢

D. 25¢

E. 11¢

F. 16¢

G. 20¢

H. 26¢

I. 9¢

Name

Comparing money   Unit 6

To compare money, use the same steps as learned before:
1. Look at the tens column.
2. If the tens column is the same, look at the ones column.

Let's go shopping! Count the money. Can you buy the item?
Circle yes or no.

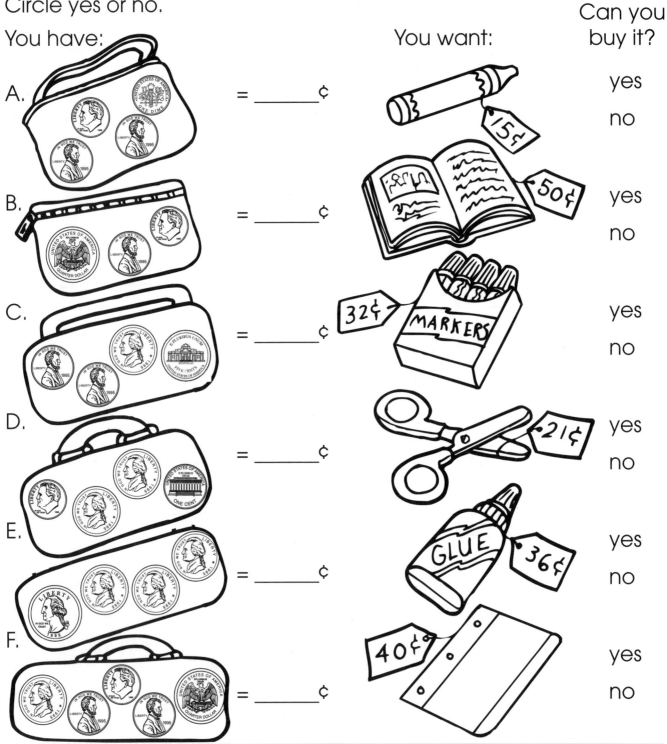

You have: You want: Can you buy it?

A.   = _____ ¢   yes
                                                           no

B.   = _____ ¢   yes
                                                           no

C.   = _____ ¢   yes
                                                           no

D.   = _____ ¢   yes
                                                           no

E.   = _____ ¢   yes
                                                           no

F.   = _____ ¢   yes
                                                           no

Name

Time to ¹/₂ hour increments   Unit 6

The short hand on a clock is called the **hour hand**.
It reads the numbers written around the clock.

The long hand is called the **minute hand**.
It does not read the numbers written
around the clock. Instead, it counts by
5s as it goes around.

8:00

8:30

Write the times.

A.
_____

B.
_____

C.
_____

D.
_____

E.
_____

F.
_____

G.
_____

H.
_____

I.
_____

J.
_____

K.
_____

L.
_____

Telling elapsed time in hours   Unit 6

Use the hour hand to tell how long something lasts. Example:

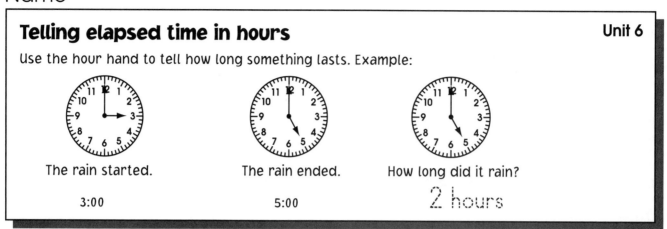

The rain started.   The rain ended.   How long did it rain?

3:00   5:00   2 hours

Find the time that has passed.

A. The sun came out at 1:00. It set at 6:00. How long was the sun out?

_____ hours

B. It began to rain at 2:00. It stopped at 4:00. How long did it rain?

_____ hours

C. The wind started at 12:00. It stopped at 3:00. How long did it blow?

_____ hours

D. The rainbow appeared at ___. It disappeared at ___. _____ hours

E. The clouds covered the sky from 5:00 until 8:00. How long did they cover the sky?

_____ hours

82   Teach & Test Math: Grade 1

Reading a calendar   Unit 6

A **calendar** shows a month of days.

February

Sun.	Mon.	Tue.	Wed.	Thur.	Fri.	Sat.
		1	2	3	4	5
6	7	8	9	10	11	12
13	14	15	16	17	18	19
20	21	22	23	24	25	26
27	28					

Use the calendar to find the answers.

A. What day is February 11? _____

B. What date is Groundhog's Day 🐻? _____

C. What date is the 2nd Tuesday? _____

D. What day is the last day of February? _____

E. What day is February 14? _____

F. How many days are in the month? _____

Name

Coins measure money. Clocks measure time. What measures weight? Let's find out!
These items are also used to measure:

 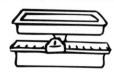 

scale   cup   thermometer   ruler
(weight)   (quantity)   (temperature)   (length)

Which would you use?

A. Suzy wants to know how heavy her box of Valentine candy is. What should she use?

B. Val wants to know how long the groundhog's shadow is. What should she use?

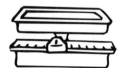

C. Alec wants to know how cold it is outside. What should he use?

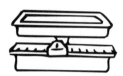

D. Mom is making cookies. She wants to add 1 cup of sugar. What should she use?

E. Eric wants to measure how long his book is. What should he use?

F. Molly wants to know if her snowman is going to melt. What should she use?

G. Ms. Johnson wants to show her class how tall Abe Lincoln was. What should she use?

H. Seth's dad is making apple pie. He needs 2 cups of flour. What should he use?

Name

Measuring length in inches   Unit 6

This is a **ruler**. It measures inches. We use it to find the length of something.

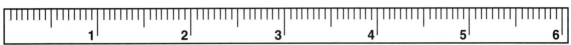

Use a ruler to find each length in inches.

A.

= _____ in.

B.

= _____ in.

C.

= _____ in.

D.

= _____ in.

E.

= _____ in.

F.

= _____ in.

  Measure the length of your foot. Then measure four other feet.
Who has the biggest feet?

Name

Some rulers measure in centimeters.

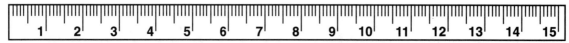

Use a ruler to find each length in centimeters.

A.

= _____ cm

B.

= _____ cm

C.

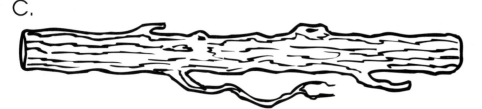

= _____ cm

D.

= _____ cm

E.

= _____ cm

F.

= _____ cm

G.

= _____ cm

Name _____

Read or listen to the question. Fill in the circle beside the best answer.

❏ Example:
Which coin is worth 5¢?

 Ⓐ   Ⓑ   Ⓒ   Ⓓ

Compare the answer choices. Some may look very similar.

Answer: D because a nickel is worth 5¢.

Now try these. You have 20 minutes. Continue until you see ⬡STOP.

---

1. Mark the dime.

 Ⓐ   Ⓑ   Ⓒ   Ⓓ

---

2. Count the coins.

Ⓐ 26¢   Ⓑ 28¢

Ⓒ 11¢   Ⓓ 6¢

---

3. Which group has 31¢?

 Ⓐ    Ⓑ   Ⓒ   Ⓓ

GO ON ⇨

4. Cole has:  Mark the item Cole can buy.

(A)   (B)   (C)   (D)

5. How long did the fair last?

Start Time   End Time

1 hour   2 hours   3 hours   4 hours

(A)   (B)   (C)   (D)

Use this calendar to answer questions 6 and 7.

June

Sun.	Mon.	Tue.	Wed.	Thur.	Fri.	Sat.
		1	2	3	4	5
6	7	8	9	10	11	12
13	14	15	16	17	18	19
20	21	22	23	24	25	26
27	28	29	30			

6. What date is the 2nd Thursday?

June 8   June 10   June 3   June 24

(A)   (B)   (C)   (D)

7. What day is June 16?

Sun.   Mon.   Tues.   Wed.

(A)   (B)   (C)   (D)

GO ON

Name

8. How many pencils are more than 4 cm long?

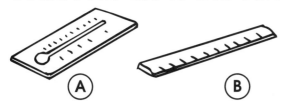

(A) 1

(B) 2

(C) 3

(D) 4

9. Josie wants to go swimming, but it may be too cold. What could Josie use to find out?

(A)   (B)   (C)   (D)

10. How long is the shoe?

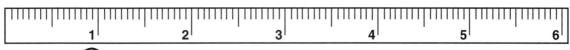

1 in. 2 in. 3 in. 4 in.

(A)   (B)   (C)   (D)

11. Which coin is worth 25¢?

(A)   (B)   (C)   (D)

12. Count the coins.

(A) 21¢   (B) 26¢

(C) 31¢   (D) 36¢

GO ON

Name

13. How much money is shown?

Ⓐ 30¢   Ⓑ 38¢

Ⓒ 48¢   Ⓓ 18

14. Which shows 11¢?

Ⓐ   Ⓑ   Ⓒ   Ⓓ

15. The girls went to the mall at 1:00. They got home at 4:00. How long did they shop?

1 hour   2 hours   3 hours   4 hours
Ⓐ   Ⓑ   Ⓒ   Ⓓ

16. Which clock shows 9:30?

Ⓐ   Ⓑ   Ⓒ   Ⓓ

17. Jamie is adding milk to make muffins. Which will she use to measure?

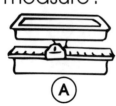  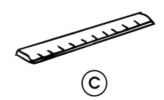 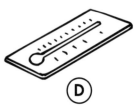

Ⓐ   Ⓑ   Ⓒ   Ⓓ

GO ON ⟹

Unit 6 Test

18. What time is it?

(A) 2:30   (B) 6:30

(C) 2:00   (D) 6:00

19. How tall is the bottle?

(A) 5 cm

(B) 6 cm

(C) 8 cm

(D) 10 cm

20. Look at the worms. Which one is about 4 inches long?

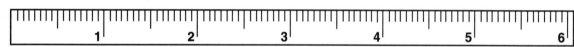

(A)

(B)

(C)

(D)

Jill needs 40 cents to buy a snack. What coins could she use? List how much each coin equals.

STOP

Name _____

Bar graph

Below is a **bar graph**. It shows the animals on the farm and the number of each. The animals are listed along the side, and one square is colored for each type of animal that Old MacDonald has.

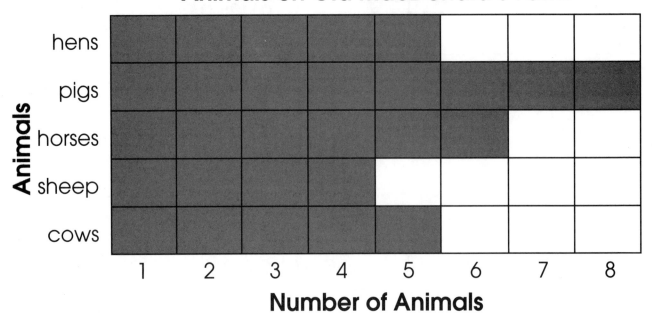

Animals on Old MacDonald's Farm

Use the bar graph to answer the questions.

A. How many cows are there on the farm? _____

B. How many pigs? _____

C. How many cows and pigs together live on the farm? _____

D. Old MacDonald has 6 _____.

E. Old MacDonald has the most _____.

F. Old MacDonald has the least _____.

G. Which two animals are the same in number?

_____ and _____

Name

This bar graph lists information across the bottom. It is not drawn into squares, but you can follow the marks to find the numbers.

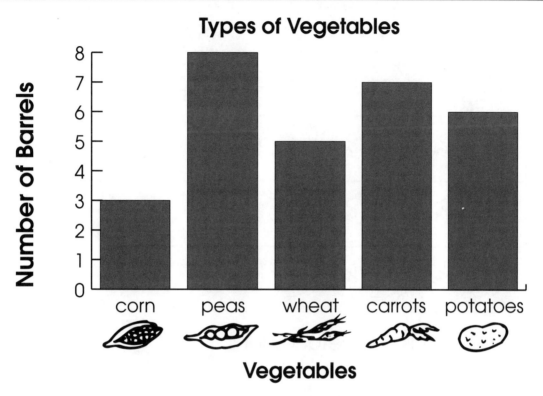

Types of Vegetables

Use the bar graph to answer the questions.

A. How many barrels of carrots and wheat altogether?

_____ + _____ = _____

B. How many more barrels of peas than wheat?

_____ – _____ = _____

C. How many barrels of corn and potatoes altogether?

_____ + _____ = _____

D. How many more barrels of carrots than potatoes?

_____ – _____ = _____

E. How many barrels of peas?

_____

F. Which crop filled 3 barrels?

_____

G. How many barrels of wheat?

_____

H. Which crop filled the most barrels?

_____

Picture graph

Picture graphs show information with small symbols. Each symbol stands for one hop on this graph.

Frog Jumping Contest

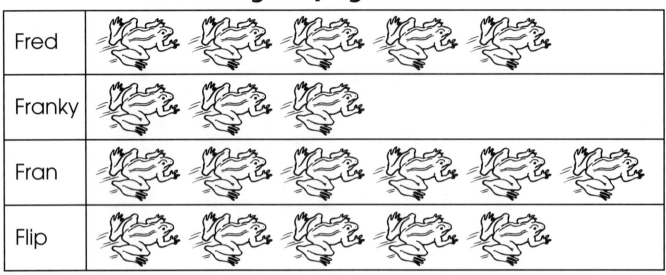

Use the graph to answer the questions.   = 1 hop

A. Which frog took 6 hops to finish the race? _____

B. Which frog took the most hops? _____

C. Which frog took the least number of hops? _____

D. How many hops did Franky take? _____

E. How many hops did Fred take? _____

F. How many hops did Flip and Fred take altogether? _____

G. Which two frogs took the same number of hops?

_____ and _____

H. How many more hops did Fran take than Flip? _____

Name

Table/chart   Unit 7

A **table** (or chart) also gives you information, but it uses numbers, rather than pictures.
This chart shows the number of toads and frogs in a pond.

In the Pond

	Monday	Tuesday	Wednesday
frogs	7	5	4
toads	6	3	8

Use the table to answer the questions.

A. On which day were there the most frogs?

_____

B. On which day were there 8 toads in the pond?

_____

C. How many toads and frogs were in the pond on Tuesday?

_____ + _____ = _____

D. How many more frogs than toads were there on Tuesday?

_____ − _____ = _____

E. How many frogs were there on all three days altogether?

_____ + _____ + _____ = _____

F. On which day were there the most frogs and toads?

_____

G. On which day were there the fewest toads?

_____

H. On which day were there 12 toads and frogs in the pond altogether?

_____

Name

Identifying equal parts

Equal parts mean pieces that are exactly the same.

These are equal parts:    These are not equal parts:

When something is divided into equal parts, we can call the parts by special names.

half   third   fourth

Two equal parts are called halves. Three equal parts are called thirds. Four equal parts are called fourths.

Color the stars that show equal parts.

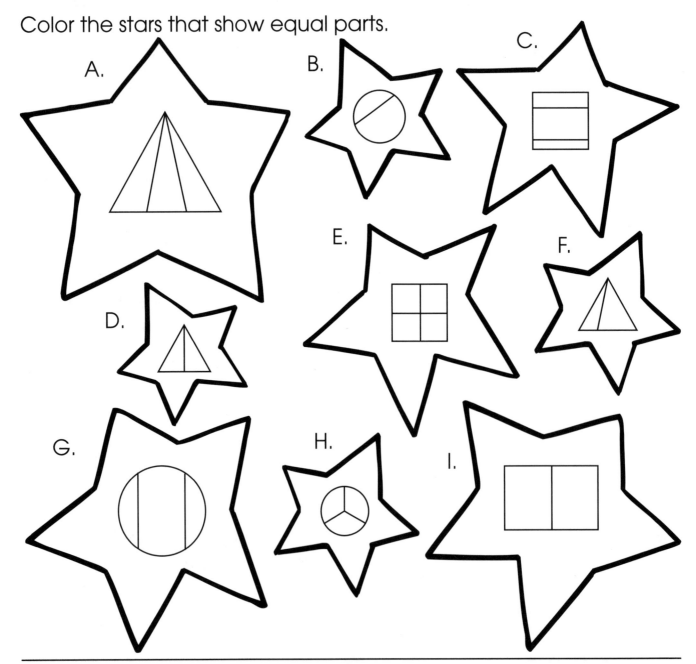

Name

Matching pictures with fractions

Equal parts can be called **fractions**. Fractions are written like this:

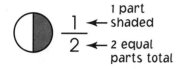 $\dfrac{1}{2}$ ← 1 part shaded
← 2 equal parts total

$\dfrac{2}{3}$ ← 2 parts shaded
← 3 equal parts total

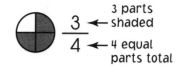 $\dfrac{3}{4}$ ← 3 parts shaded
← 4 equal parts total

Circle the fraction that matches the shaded picture on each rocket.

A.
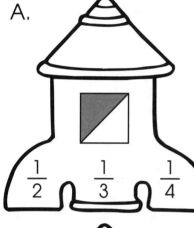
$\dfrac{1}{2}$ $\dfrac{1}{3}$ $\dfrac{1}{4}$

B.
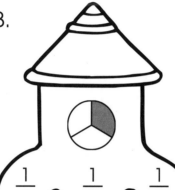
$\dfrac{1}{2}$ $\dfrac{1}{3}$ $\dfrac{1}{4}$

C.
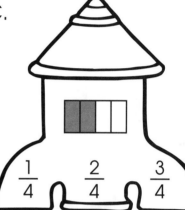
$\dfrac{1}{4}$ $\dfrac{2}{4}$ $\dfrac{3}{4}$

D.
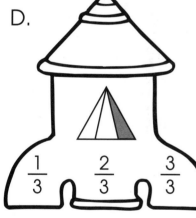
$\dfrac{1}{3}$ $\dfrac{2}{3}$ $\dfrac{3}{3}$

E.
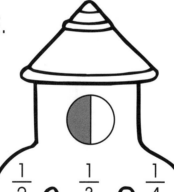
$\dfrac{1}{2}$ $\dfrac{1}{3}$ $\dfrac{1}{4}$

F.
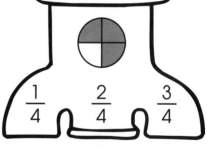
$\dfrac{1}{4}$ $\dfrac{2}{4}$ $\dfrac{3}{4}$

G.
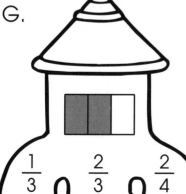
$\dfrac{1}{3}$ $\dfrac{2}{3}$ $\dfrac{2}{4}$

H.
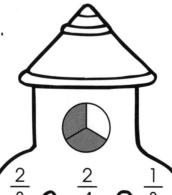
$\dfrac{2}{3}$ $\dfrac{2}{4}$ $\dfrac{1}{3}$

I.
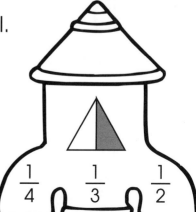
$\dfrac{1}{4}$ $\dfrac{1}{3}$ $\dfrac{1}{2}$

Name

Illustrating given fractions

Remember this:

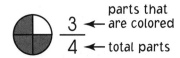

$\dfrac{3}{4}$ ← parts that are colored / total parts

Color each picture to match the given fraction.

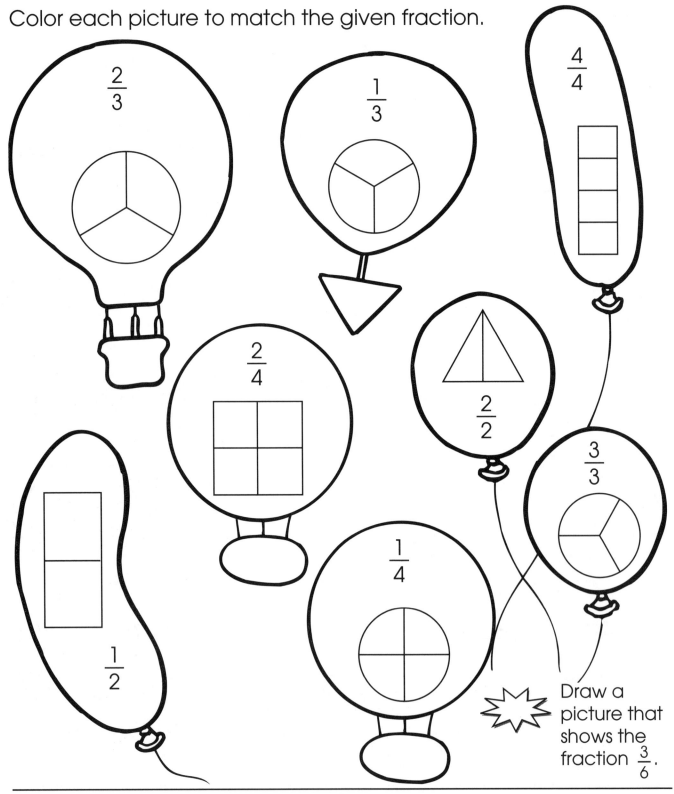

Draw a picture that shows the fraction $\dfrac{3}{6}$.

Name

Illustrating part of a group as a fraction

Like equal parts, members of a similar group can be described as a fraction.

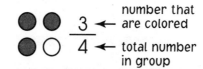

$\dfrac{3}{4}$ ← number that are colored
← total number in group

Color the spring picture to match these fractions:

$\dfrac{2}{3}$ of the birds are blue.

$\dfrac{3}{4}$ of the trees have nests.

$\dfrac{1}{4}$ of the butterflies are orange.

$\dfrac{1}{2}$ of the children have a kite.

$\dfrac{2}{4}$ of the flowers are yellow.

$\dfrac{1}{3}$ of the birds are red.

$\dfrac{3}{4}$ of the butterflies are purple.

Name

Read or listen to the question. Fill in the circle beside the best answer.

☐ Example:
Which group shows $\frac{2}{3}$ black?

(A) (B) (C) (D)

Use your time wisely. If a problem seems tough, skip it and come back to it later.

Answer: A because it has a total of 3 balls with 2 of them black.

Now try these. You have 20 minutes. Continue until you see .

---

1. Which shows half of the triangle shaded?

(A) (B) (C) (D)

---

2. Which fraction matches the picture?

$\frac{2}{4}$ $\frac{1}{4}$ $\frac{1}{3}$ $\frac{4}{2}$

(A) (B) (C) (D)

---

3. Which picture shows $\frac{3}{4}$ of the birds in a nest?

(A) (B) (C) (D)

GO ON ▷

4. Which picture matches the fraction?

$\dfrac{1}{4}$ Ⓐ $\dfrac{1}{3}$ Ⓑ $\dfrac{3}{1}$ Ⓒ $\dfrac{2}{4}$ Ⓓ

Use this picture graph to answer questions 5–8.

Tulips in Our School Greenhouse

yellow	🌷 🌷 🌷 🌷 🌷 🌷
pink	🌷 🌷 🌷 🌷 🌷
red	🌷 🌷 🌷 🌷 🌷 🌷 🌷
white	🌷 🌷 🌷

🌷 = 1 tulip plant

5. The most tulips are what color?

yellow Ⓐ   pink Ⓑ   red Ⓒ   white Ⓓ

6. How many pink and red tulips are there altogether?

11 Ⓐ   12 Ⓑ   10 Ⓒ   9 Ⓓ

7. How many more red tulips are there than white?

$7 - 3 = 4$ Ⓐ $6 - 4 = 2$ Ⓑ $7 - 6 = 1$ Ⓒ $6 - 5 = 1$ Ⓓ

8. Which color has 5 tulips?

yellow Ⓐ   pink Ⓑ   red Ⓒ   white Ⓓ

GO ON

Name

Use this bar graph to answer questions 9–12.

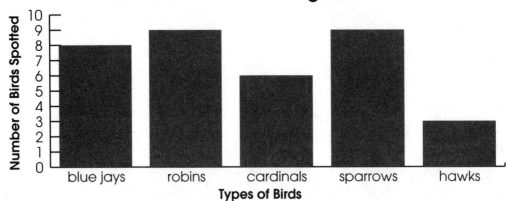

Bird Watching

9. The class spotted 8 _____.

    blue jays   robins   sparrows   hawks
      (A)   (B)   (C)   (D)

10. How many more robins than cardinals were seen?

       1   2   3   4
      (A)   (B)   (C)   (D)

11. How many blue jays and cardinals together were seen?

    8 + 3 = 11   9 + 9 = 18   7 + 1 = 8   8 + 6 = 14
      (A)   (B)   (C)   (D)

12. Which two birds did the class see the same number?

    (A) blue jays and cardinals   (B) blue jays and robins

    (C) robins and sparrows   (D) sparrows and hawks

GO ON

Use this table to answer questions 13–16.

Stars Earned for Hard Work

	reading	writing	math
Room 5	12	9	10
Room 6	11	10	8
Room 7	8	12	9
Room 8	10	8	11

13. Which room earned the most stars in writing?

Room 5
Ⓐ

Room 6
Ⓑ

Room 7
Ⓒ

Room 8
Ⓓ

14. How many stars in math did Rooms 5 and 7 earn altogether?

19
Ⓐ

21
Ⓑ

9
Ⓒ

11
Ⓓ

15. How many stars did Room 6 earn in reading and writing altogether?

9 + 9
Ⓐ

11 + 10
Ⓑ

10 + 8
Ⓒ

8 + 12
Ⓓ

16. How many more stars in reading did Room 6 earn than Room 8?

12 – 10
Ⓐ

10 – 8
Ⓑ

12 – 8
Ⓒ

11 – 10
Ⓓ

GO ON

Unit 7 Test

17. Which circle shows 3 equal parts?

Ⓐ

Ⓑ

Ⓒ

Ⓓ

18. Which shaded picture matches the fraction?

$\dfrac{2}{3}$

Ⓐ

Ⓑ

Ⓒ

Ⓓ

19. Which picture shows thirds?

Ⓐ

Ⓑ

Ⓒ

Ⓓ

20. Which picture shows $\dfrac{2}{4}$ of the dogs sleeping?

Ⓐ

Ⓑ

Ⓒ

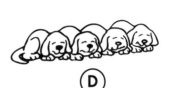
Ⓓ

Mrs. Franklin asked her class what their favorite color was. The results were:

blue–6   red–3   green–4

Make a bar graph using this information.

STOP

Name

Matching illustrations with word problems

Did you know that you can read some math problems, just the way you read a book?
There may even be pictures to go along with the story.

Cut out the pictures at the bottom of the page and glue them with their matching story problem.

A. There are 3 apples on the tree. 5 more apples are on the ground. How many apples in all?	B. The table has 9 markers. Jill brings 2 more. How many markers are there now?
C. There are 7 scissors in our room. Our teacher gave us 8 more. How many scissors are there now?	D. Ms. Morton has 6 apples on her desk. Her students bring her 3 more. How many apples are there now?
E. Yakim has 8 markers. CheLei has 3 markers. How many do they have together?	F. There are 6 scissors at the art center. 6 more are at the math center. How many scissors are there in all?

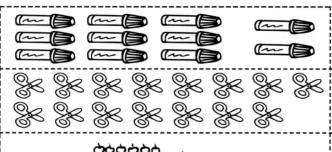

Identifying key addition words

Unit 8

Each of the stories has a question at the end. Your job is to find the answer using key words that tell you to add. These words are: *altogether*, *total*, *in all*, and *combined*.

Circle the key words in each story. Then write an addition problem to find the answer.

A. Annie counted 6 red and 12 blue crayons. How many total crayons did Annie count?

B. Lauren has 8 orange and 7 red crayons. How many crayons does she have in all?

C. Clay counted 41 green and 13 brown crayons. How many is that altogether?

D. Sally counted 15 yellow and 21 pink crayons. How many crayons is that combined?

E. Cal counted 27 black and 20 red crayons. How many total crayons did Cal count?

F. Bret counted 32 blue and 34 green crayons. How many did he count in all?

G. P.J. counted 51 purple and 32 gray crayons. How many did he count altogether?

H. David has 6 pink and 5 yellow crayons. How many does he have combined?

Name

Matching illustrations with subtraction word problems   Unit 8

Some stories start with a big group and a few things are taken away. Stories like this tell you to subtract.

Cut out the pictures at the bottom of the page. Glue them with their matching stories. Then find the answers.

A. Juan has 8 coins. He trades 4 of them away. How many are left?	B. Corey has 10 coins. He lost 3 of them. How many does he have left?
C. Darby has 13 coins. She trades 5 of them away. How many are left?	D. Mei Lee has 6 coins. She gives 2 of them away. How many does she have now?
E. Mark has 11 coins. He lost 6. How many coins does Mark have now?	F. Denell has 12 coins. He gives 6 a them to a friend. How many are left?
G. Margarite has 5 coins. She gives 2 to her sister. How many does she have now?	H. Shanise has 9 coins. She lost 4 on her way to school. How many does she have now?

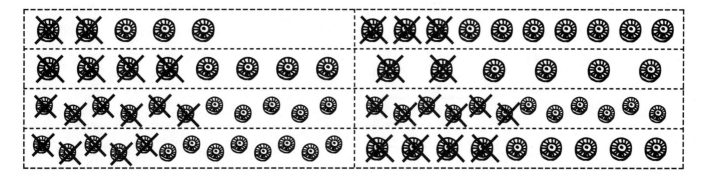

Identifying key subtraction words

Unit 8

There are some key words that tell you to subtract in story problems. They are: *have left*, *how many more*, and *difference*.

Our class has worked hard to earn reward stickers. We keep them grouped into categories:

Dinosaurs 32	Animals 45	Plants 20
Airplanes 67	Sports 99	Trucks 89

Use the chart to find the numbers you need for each story. Then circle the key words that tell you to subtract. Finally, find the answer.

A. How many more airplane than animal stickers are there?

B. What is the difference between dinosaur and truck stickers?

C. What is the difference between sports and airplane stickers?

D. The class has 67 airplane stickers. They may give 13 away. How many will be left?

E. How many more truck stickers than plant stickers are there?

Write your own problem using the chart.

Name

Choosing to add or subtract in word problems

Unit 8

Story problems can also tell about the cost of something. There are key words to help with these problems:

add = *in all, altogether, combined, total*
subtract = *how much more, difference*

The first-graders in Ms. Ryan's class are selling baked goods. Use the prices below to solve the story problems. Circle the key words to help you decide to add or subtract.

A. How much more is a cake than cookies?	☐	☐☐ ¢ ☐☐ ¢ ——— ☐☐ ¢	B. How much would two brownies cost in all?	☐	☐☐ ¢ ☐☐ ¢ ——— ☐☐ ¢
C. How much do cupcakes and cookies cost altogether?	☐	☐☐ ¢ ☐☐ ¢ ——— ☐☐ ¢	D. How much more is a cake than the cupcakes?	☐	☐☐ ¢ ☐☐ ¢ ——— ☐☐ ¢
E. What is the total cost of muffins and cookies?	☐	☐☐ ¢ ☐☐ ¢ ——— ☐☐ ¢	F. What is the difference in the cost of a cake and muffins?	☐	☐☐ ¢ ☐☐ ¢ ——— ☐☐ ¢

Name

Choosing to add or subtract

Remember the key words you have learned. They will help you find the answers to these shopping story problems.

Use the bake sale prices on page 109 to write an addition or subtraction problem. Then find the answers.

A. Kayla has 99¢. She buys a cake. How much does she have left?	B. Eric buys a cake and brownies. How much does he spend in all?
C. Zoe has 67¢, She buys some muffins. How much does she have left?	D. Kurt has 93¢. He buys some cookies. How much does he have left?
E. Jimmy buys cupcakes and brownies. How much does he spend total?	F. Haley buys muffins and cupcakes. How much does she spend altogether?
G. Michael has 83¢. He buys some cookies. How much money does he have left?	H. Devon has 88¢. She buys a cake. How much does she have left?

Name

Sometimes story problems seem to leave out some information. You can find the missing information by drawing a picture or writing a math problem.

Write a math problem to find the answer to each question below.

A. Twelve kids are playing on the swings. Seven of them are boys. How many girls are playing on the swings?	B. A family drives 14 miles to the beach. Then they drive home. How many total miles did the family drive?
C. The farmer's horse eats 3 buckets of food each day. How many buckets will he eat in two days?	D. Brittney is 8 years old. Her brother is 5 years older. How old is Brittney's brother?
E. The cage holds 12 birds. Eight of them are black. How many are not black?	F. Eighteen kids began climbing the rope. Nine of them made it to the top. How many did not make it to the top?

Using pictures to problem solve

Unit 8

To find the answer to a riddle, follow these steps:

1. Read the clue.
2. Put an X on the pictures that cannot be the answer.
3. Continue until one picture is left.

1. I am not a pet.

2. I do not have stripes.

3. I am black. What number am I? _____

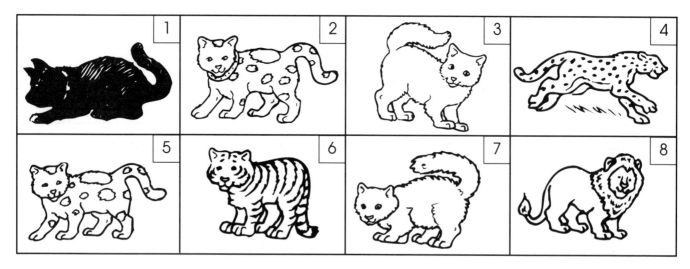

1. I am a house pet.

2. I do not have a collar on.

3. I have spots. What number am I? _____

    112

Unit 8 Test

Problem Solving

Read or listen to the question. Fill in the circle beside the best answer.

Read the question again. Does your answer make sense?

❑ Example:
There are 10 cats in the yard.
Three of them went in the sandbox.
How many are left in the yard?

Mark the number sentence that will help you find the answer.

$10 > 3$ $3 < 10$ $10 + 3 = \square$ $10 - 3 = \square$
Ⓐ   Ⓑ   Ⓒ   Ⓓ

Answer: D because "are left" tells you to subtract.

Now try these. You have 20 minutes. Continue until you see .

---

1. Juanita has 21 books about animals. She has 14 books about sports. How many books does Juanita have total?

   53   35   39   7
   Ⓐ   Ⓑ   Ⓒ   Ⓓ

---

2. There are lots of fish in our pond. We saw 6 gold, 4 red, and 3 blue fish. How many fish did we see in all?

6	gold
4	red
3	blue

   10   7   9   13
   Ⓐ   Ⓑ   Ⓒ   Ⓓ

GO ON ▷

---

3. A bakery has 37 cupcakes. They sell 14 of them. How many cupcakes are left? Mark the number sentence that would help you find the answer.

37 – 14 = ☐   37 + 14 = ☐   37 > 14   14 < 37
Ⓐ   Ⓑ   Ⓒ   Ⓓ

4. Forty-six tulips and 23 roses grew in our garden. How many flowers are there altogether? Mark the number sentence that would help you find the answer.

46 – 23 = ☐   46 > 32   46 + 23 = ☐   23 < 46
Ⓐ   Ⓑ   Ⓒ   Ⓓ

5. Jacob ate 11 cookies. Bailey ate 6 cookies. How many more cookies did Jacob eat?

Ⓐ   Ⓑ   Ⓒ   Ⓓ

6. Mark the picture that matches the story.

Tayla has 5 beads on her bracelet. Her sister gives her 2 more beads. How many beads does Tayla have altogether?

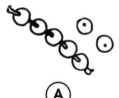   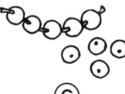   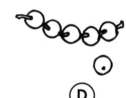
Ⓐ   Ⓑ   Ⓒ   Ⓓ

GO ON ▷

7. Jenna is 10 years old. Her brother is 4 years younger. How old is Jenna's brother. Which number sentence would help you find the answer?

$10 + 4 = \square$ $10 - 4 = \square$ $10 > 4$ $4 < 10$
Ⓐ   Ⓑ   Ⓒ   Ⓓ

8. Chelsea picked 18 apples. She gave 9 to her teacher and brought the others home. How many apples did Chelsea bring home?

6   7   8   9
Ⓐ   Ⓑ   Ⓒ   Ⓓ

9. Mark the boy that answers the riddle:

1. I have curly hair.
2. I am wearing stripes.

Ⓐ   Ⓑ   Ⓒ   Ⓓ

10. Mark the number sentence that matches the picture.

Ⓐ $8 + 4 = \square$

Ⓑ $5 + 6 = \square$

Ⓒ $3 + 8 = \square$

Ⓓ $5 + 3 = \square$

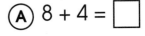

11. Which picture shows how many more forks there are than spoons?

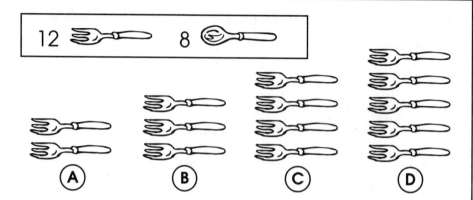

    Ⓐ   Ⓑ   Ⓒ   Ⓓ

12. A dentist has 45 toothbrushes. He gives 31 away. How many toothbrushes does he have left? Mark the number sentence that would help you find the answer.

$45 + 31 = \square$ $45 - 31 = \square$ $31 < 45$ $45 > 31$
  Ⓐ   Ⓑ   Ⓒ   Ⓓ

13. Mark the picture that matches the story. Mom made 14 tacos for dinner. We ate 9 of them. How many tacos were left?

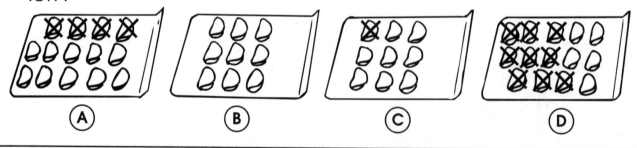

    Ⓐ   Ⓑ   Ⓒ   Ⓓ

14. A.J. had 45¢. He made his bed and earned 44¢ more. How much money does A.J. have altogether?

    45¢   89¢   44¢   62¢
    Ⓐ   Ⓑ   Ⓒ   Ⓓ

GO ON

15. Seth bought a pencil for 15¢. He bought an eraser for 8¢. How much more was the pencil? Which number sentence would help you find the answer?

18¢ > 15¢   15¢ − 8¢ = ☐   15¢ < 18¢   15¢ + 8¢ = ☐
Ⓐ   Ⓑ   Ⓒ   Ⓓ

16. My dog had 10 puppies. Three of them were black. How many were not black? Mark the number sentence that would help you find the answer.

3 < 10   10 + 3 = ☐   10 > 3   10 − 3 = ☐
Ⓐ   Ⓑ   Ⓒ   Ⓓ

17. Tara planted 16 seeds. Nine of them grew. How many did not grow? Mark the number sentence that would help you find the answer.

16 − 9 = ☐   16 + 9 = ☐   9 < 16   16 > 9
Ⓐ   Ⓑ   Ⓒ   Ⓓ

18. Find the answer to the riddle.

I do not have stripes. I have horns. I am spotted.

Ⓐ

Ⓑ

Ⓒ   Ⓓ

GO ON ⟩

19. Seventeen students are in Mr. Sander's class. Four are absent. How many students are in class today?

17 + 4 = 21	14 − 7 = 7	17 − 4 = 13	17 − 14 = 3
Ⓐ	Ⓑ	Ⓒ	Ⓓ

20. Casey had 25¢. He bought some gum for 12¢. How much money did Casey have left?

37¢	23¢	13¢	47¢
Ⓐ	Ⓑ	Ⓒ	Ⓓ

Write a word problem using the numbers 6 and 9. Solve the problem.

STOP

Name

Read or listen to the question. Use an extra piece of paper to work on problems. Fill in the circle beside the best answer completely and neatly.

❏ Example:

Which measures temperature?

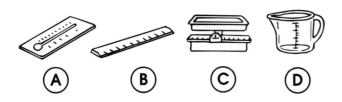

Ⓐ   Ⓑ   Ⓒ   Ⓓ

Answer: A because a thermometer measures temperature.

Now try these. You have 35 minutes.

Continue until you see ⬡STOP⬡.

Remember your Helping Hand Strategies:

 1. When using scratch paper, copy carefully.

 2. Compare the answer choices. Some may look very similar.

 3. Use your time wisely. If something seems tough, skip it and come back to it later.

 4. Read the question again. Does your answer make sense?

1. How many blocks are there?

523   532   205   352
Ⓐ   Ⓑ   Ⓒ   Ⓓ

2. Which shape has five sides?

Ⓐ   Ⓑ   Ⓒ   Ⓓ

GO ON ⟹

Use this bar graph to answer questions 3–5.

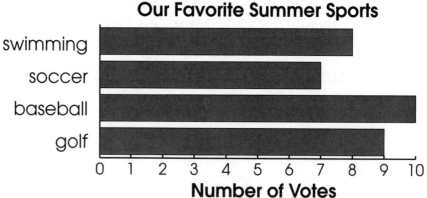

Our Favorite Summer Sports

Sports: swimming, soccer, baseball, golf

Number of Votes (0 1 2 3 4 5 6 7 8 9 10)

3. How many more kids voted for baseball than soccer?

2
Ⓐ

3
Ⓑ

4
Ⓒ

5
Ⓓ

4. How many votes did golf and swimming get combined?

12
Ⓐ

14
Ⓑ

15
Ⓒ

17
Ⓓ

5. Which sport is the least favorite?

soccer
Ⓐ

swimming
Ⓑ

baseball
Ⓒ

golf
Ⓓ

6. Which number sentence shows how many more shoes there are than socks?

$8 + 4 = \square$
Ⓐ

$12 - 8 = \square$
Ⓑ

$8 - 4 = \square$
Ⓒ

$6 - 2 = \square$
Ⓓ

GO ON →

7. How many strings are more than 3 inches long?

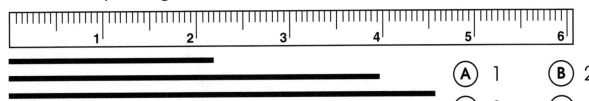

(A) 1   (B) 2

(C) 3   (D) 4

8. Which number is the lowest?

24	48	29	51
(A)	(B)	(C)	(D)

9.
$$\begin{array}{r} 15 \\ -\ \ 8 \\ \hline \end{array}$$

eight   seven   six   five
(A)   (B)   (C)   (D)

10. Jude has the coins shown. Mark the item he can buy.

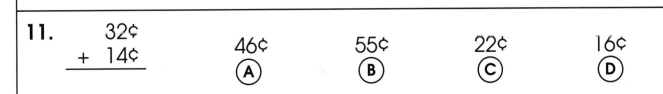

(A)   (B)   (C)   (D)

11.
$$\begin{array}{r} 32¢ \\ +\ 14¢ \\ \hline \end{array}$$

46¢   55¢   22¢   16¢
(A)   (B)   (C)   (D)

12. What number is missing? 55, 60, 65, _____, 75

66   68   70   72
(A)   (B)   (C)   (D)

GO ON

Final Review Test

13. Which shows half the circle shaded?

Ⓐ   Ⓑ   Ⓒ   Ⓓ

14. Yasmin collected 9 rocks on Monday. She found 8 more on Tuesday. How many rocks does she have in all?

$9 + 8 = 17$ $7 + 7 = 14$ $9 - 8 = 1$ $17 + 3 = 20$
    Ⓐ   Ⓑ   Ⓒ   Ⓓ

15. Finish the pattern.

Ⓐ   Ⓑ   Ⓒ   Ⓓ

16. Which of the other half of this shape?

             Ⓐ   Ⓑ   Ⓒ   Ⓓ

17. Mom needs 2 pounds of potatoes. Which should she use to measure?

Ⓐ   Ⓑ   Ⓒ   Ⓓ

GO ON

Teach & Test Math: Grade 1

Name

18.
264
+ 514

807 (A) 778 (B) 780 (C) 87 (D)

19.
738
- 512

206 (A) 226 (B) 620 (C) 240 (D)

20. Count the coins.

(A) 16¢   (B) 46¢

(C) 36¢   (D) 28¢

21. Which **does not** show 99?

T	O
9	9

(A)

ninety-nine (B)   100 – 1 (C)   9 + 9 (D)

22.
89
- 43

16 (A)   26 (B)   36 (C)   46 (D)

23. Tasha saw 32 stars one night and 46 the next night. How many stars did Tasha see altogether? Mark the number sentence that would help you find the answer.

32 + 46 = ☐ (A)   46 – 32 = ☐ (B)   46 > 32 (C)   32 < 46 (D)

GO ON ⇨

Name

24. Which number sentence matches the picture?

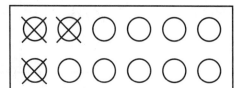

Ⓐ 12 – 3 = 9

Ⓑ 12 + 3 = 15

Ⓒ 3 + 6 = 9

Ⓓ 10 – 4 = 6

25. How long did the movie last?

Start Time  End Time

Ⓐ 1 hour

Ⓑ 2 hours

Ⓒ 3 hours

Ⓓ 4 hours

26. I am < 36. What am I?

65	50	40	25
Ⓐ	Ⓑ	Ⓒ	Ⓓ

27. Marji had 16 cupcakes for her birthday. Nine of them were iced. How many cupcakes were not iced? Mark the number sentence that would help you find the answer.

16 + 9 = ☐   16 – 9 = ☐   16 > 9   9 – 16 = ☐
  Ⓐ   Ⓑ   Ⓒ   Ⓓ

28. Which clock shows 9:30?

 Ⓐ   Ⓑ   Ⓒ   Ⓓ

GO ON ➡

Final Review Test

29. Which **does not** equal 6?

$15 - 9$	$14 - 8$	$13 - 7$	$12 - 5$
Ⓐ	Ⓑ	Ⓒ	Ⓓ

30. Which number sentence is true?

$4 + 7 = 13$	$8 + 6 = 14$	$7 + 7 = 15$	$4 + 5 = 10$
Ⓐ	Ⓑ	Ⓒ	Ⓓ

Brent has 78 baseball cards. Kevin has 34 baseball cards. How many more cards does Brent have than Kevin? Solve the problem. Show three ways you could write the answer.

STOP

Answer Key

Page 5
Check students' pages.

Page 6
A. 9; B. 10; C. 8; D. 20; E. 14; F. 13; G. 15; H. 16; I. 14; J. 14

Page 7
A. 3, 2, 1, 4; B. 4, 3, 2, 1; C. 3, 1, 4, 2; D. 3, 1, 4, 2; E. 4, 3, 2, 1; F. 3, 1, 2, 4

Page 8
Check students' pages.

Page 9
Check students' pages.

Page 10
A. 13, 46, 83, 71, 27, 80, 99, 81, 30; B. 81, 7, 30, 50, 12, 73, 59, 21, 65, 39; C. 98, 27, 66, 79, 9, 99, 35, 77, 51, 89

Page 11
A. Circle third box. Put an X on second box.; B. Circle first box. Put an X on third box.; C. Circle second box. Put an X on first box.; D. Circle first box. Put an X on second box. Last three boxes—check students' answers.

Page 12
A. >; B. >; C. <; D. <; E. >; F. <; G. >; H. =

Page 13
Check students' pages.

Page 14
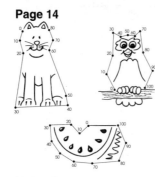

Unit 1 Test
1. B; 2. C; 3. A; 4. D; 5. D; 6. A; 7. B; 8. C; 9. A; 10. D; 11. C; 12. B; 13. A; 14. C; 15. D; 16. A; 17. B; 18. B; 19. A; 20. B; Constructed-response answers will vary.

Page 20
Check students' pages for circles. A. 16; B. 13; C. 19; D. 10; E. 15; F. 18; G. 14; H. 17

Page 21
A. 43; B. 57; C. 86; D. 62; E. 34; F. 95; G. 70; H. 27; I. 59

Page 22
A. 63; B. 29; C. 46; D. 92; E. 57; F. 70; G. 81

Page 23
Check students' pages.

Page 24
A. 351; B. 624; C. 285; D. 703; E. 539; F. 420; G. 191

Page 25
Check students' page.

Page 26
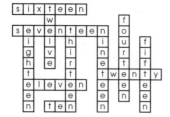

Page 27

eighty-six = 86; ninety-one = 91; forty-five = 45; sixty-two = 62; seventy-four = 74; seventy-five = 75; twenty-one = 21; thirteen = 13; thirty = 30; forty-nine = 49; fifty-six = 56; fifty-eight = 58; ninety = 90; nineteen = 19; eighty-four = 84; eighty-five = 85; sixty-seven = 67; seventy-six = 76

Page 28
A. <; B. >; C. >; D. <; E. >; F. >; G. <; H. >; I. <; J. <

Page 29
A. 15; B. 27; C. 92; D. 30; E. 46; F. 8; G. 57; H. 76

Unit 2 Test
1. A; 2. C; 3. D; 4. B; 5. A; 6. C; 7. B; 8. A; 9. D; 10. D; 11. B; 12. A; 13. C; 14. C; 15. D; 16. B; 17. A; 18. B; 19. A; 20. C; Constructed-response answers will vary.

Page 34
triangle: 3, 18; square: 4, 6; rectangle: 4, 7; circle: 0, 6; oval: 0, 2

Page 35
Students should color the bowling ball red, the jack-in-the-box blue, the handheld game yellow, the kaleidoscope orange, the top green, and the triangle purple.

Page 36

Page 37
Check students' drawings.

Page 38

Page 39
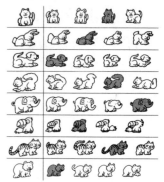

Page 40

Page 41
A. 1, 2, 4, 3; B. 2, 4, 3, 1; C. 2, 1, 4, 3; D. 2, 4, 1, 3; E. 1, 3, 4, 2

Answer Key

Unit 3 Test

1. B; 2. D; 3. B; 4. B; 5. C; 6. A; 7. B; 8. C; 9. D; 10. D; 11. A; 12. D; 13. C; 14. C; 15. B; 16. D; 17. D; 18. C; 19. A; 20. C; Constructed response: Answers may vary. They both have 4 sides. The rectangle has 2 sides that are longer.

Page 47

A. 6; B. 9; C. 10; D. 6; E. 9; F. 10; G. 10; H. 10; I. 8; J. 9; K. 7

Page 48

A. 4 + 3 = 7; B. 5 + 4 = 9; C. 5 + 5 = 10; D. 1 + 2 = 3; E. 5 + 2 = 7; F. 5 + 4 = 9; G. 7 + 1 = 8; H. 2 + 5 = 7; I. 3 + 3 = 6;
J. 3 + 6 = 9; K. 7 + 3 = 10; L. 2 + 4 = 6

Page 49

A. 11; B. 12; C. 12; D. 14; E. 12; F. 12; G. 11; H. 11; I. 13; J. 13; K. 11; L. 13; M. 11; N. 14; O. 14

Page 50

$\frac{3}{+9}$ 12	$\frac{3}{+4}$ 7	$\frac{8}{+1}$ 9	$\frac{2}{+2}$ 4	
$\frac{4}{+8}$ 12	$\frac{6}{+7}$ 13	$\frac{3}{+6}$ 9	$\frac{4}{+4}$ 8	$\frac{6}{+0}$ 6
$\frac{6}{+6}$ 12	$\frac{5}{+4}$ 9	$\frac{7}{+2}$ 9	$\frac{3}{+3}$ 6	$\frac{4}{+2}$ 6
$\frac{9}{+2}$ 11	$\frac{7}{+7}$ 14	$\frac{8}{+5}$ 13	$\frac{3}{+8}$ 11	$\frac{7}{+4}$ 11
$\frac{7}{+2}$ 9	$\frac{1}{+8}$ 9	$\frac{4}{+5}$ 9	$\frac{6}{+3}$ 9	$\frac{4}{+9}$ 13
$\frac{7}{+6}$ 13	$\frac{8}{+4}$ 12	$\frac{7}{+7}$ 14	$\frac{5}{+7}$ 12	$\frac{6}{+5}$ 11

Page 51

RIVER BANK
E. 11; I. 12; C. 9; N. 13; R. 17; L. 10; P. 8; B. 14; A. 16; V. 15; S. 7; K. 18

Page 52

A. 12; B. 15; C. 14; D. 16; E. 16; F. 18; G. 14; H. 14; I. 9; J. 3; K. 12; L. 16; M. 8; N. 10; O. 17; P. 13; Q. 15; R. 9

Page 53

A. 7 + 5 + 3 = 15; B. 4 + 5 + 5 = 14; C. 4 + 5 + 8 = 17; D. 9 + 5 + 4 = 18; E. 4 + 5 + 7 = 16; F. 4 + 5 + 4 = 13; G. 4 + 5 + 3 = 12; H. 4 + 5 + 5 = 14; I. 7 + 5 + 2 = 14; J. 1 + 5 + 3 = 9; K. 3 + 5 + 8 = 16; L. 8 + 5 + 4 = 17

Page 54

$\frac{35}{+34}$ 69 $\frac{42}{+51}$ 93 $\frac{63}{+24}$ 87 $\frac{17}{+32}$ 49 $\frac{76}{+12}$ 88 $\frac{42}{+30}$ 72

$\frac{32}{+21}$ 53 $\frac{61}{+30}$ 91 $\frac{33}{+31}$ 64 $\frac{25}{+13}$ 38 $\frac{30}{+40}$ 70 $\frac{24}{+32}$ 56

$\frac{35}{+2}$ 37 $\frac{23}{+22}$ 45 $\frac{32}{+35}$ 67 $\frac{61}{+31}$ 92 $\frac{50}{+30}$ 80

Page 55

A. 987; B. 691; C. 932; D. 799; E. 778; F. 861; G. 875; H. 749; I. 989; J. 947; K. 966; L. 959; M. 767; N. 898

Unit 4 Test

1. C; 2. B; 3. B; 4. A; 5. A; 6. B; 7. D; 8. C; 9. A; 10. B; 11. B; 12. D; 13. A; 14. C; 15. D; 16. B; 17. C; 18. A; 19. D; 20. A; Constructed-response answers will vary.

Midway Review Test

1. C; 2. A; 3. D; 4. B; 5. C; 6. A; 7. B; 8. B; 9. A; 10. D; 11. C; 12. B; 13. B; 14. C; 15. A; 16. B; 17. D; 18. A; 19. D; 20. D; Constructed-response answers will vary.

Page 64

A. 5, 5, 6, 6; B. 5, 4, 3, 4; C. 3, 2, 4, 4; D. 3, 2, 5, 6

Page 65

9 − 3 = 6, 8 − 4 = 4, 10 − 6 = 4, 7 − 3 = 4, 9 − 4 = 5, 6 − 3 = 3; 8 − 3 = 5, 10 − 5 = 5, 9 − 2 = 7, 7 − 2 = 5, 10 − 4 = 6, 8 − 5 = 3

Page 66

A. 8, B. 7, C. 6, D. 7, E. 3, F. 8, G. 6, H. 6, I. 4, J. 4, K. 9, L. 6

Page 67

A. 8, 6, 7, 5; B. 5, 8, 4, 7; C. 4, 4, 9, 7; D. 5, 6, 6, 7; E. 3, 6, 9, 5

Page 68

A. 5 + 7 = 12, 7 + 5 = 12, 12 − 5 = 7, 12 − 7 = 5; B. 7 + 8 = 15, 8 + 7 = 15, 15 − 7 = 8, 15 − 8 = 7; C. 8 + 9 = 17, 9 + 8 = 17, 17 − 8 = 9, 17 − 9 = 8; D. 6 + 8 = 14, 8 + 6 = 14, 14 − 6 = 8, 14 − 8 = 6

Page 69

A. 7, 9, 9, 5, 8; B. 9, 7, 9, 8, 5; C. 7, 6, 6, 8, 7; D. 6, 7, 8

Page 70

THEY BOTH HAVE A CRUST!

O. 7; E. 9; C. 16; A. 4; Y. 6; T. 18; S. 17; R. 14; H. 8; U. 11; V. 5; B. 15

Page 71

A. 23, 53, 42, 66, 51, 45; B. 44, 12, 52, 43, 12, 53; C. 11, 42, 34, 26, 33, 52

Page 72

2,661

A. 222, 332, 631, 346; B. 255, 342, 464, 266; C. 411, 621, 204, 316

Unit 5 Test

1. C; 2. A; 3. D; 4. B; 5. D; 6. C; 7. A; 8. D; 9. B; 10. A; 11. C; 12. A; 13. B; 14. C; 15. B; 16. A; 17. D; 18. B; 19. A; 20. C; Constructed-response answers will vary.

Page 77

A. 11¢; B. 10¢; C. 3¢; D. 7¢; E. 16¢; F. 15¢; G. 4¢; H. 10¢; I. 15¢

Page 78

A. 26¢; B. 25¢; C. 25¢; D. 14¢; E. 5¢; F. 21¢; G. 16¢; H. 27¢

Page 79

Answers may vary.

Page 80

A. 22¢, yes; B. 36¢, no; C. 12¢, no; D. 21¢, yes; E. 40¢, yes; F. 42¢, yes

Page 81

A. 2:30; B. 1:00; C. 4:30; D. 8:00; E. 3:30; F. 11:00; G. 9:30; H. 12:00; I. 6:30; J. 7:30; K. 12:30; L. 6:00

Page 82

A. 5; B. 2; C. 3; D. 2; E. 3

Page 83

A. Friday; B. February 2; C. 8; D. Monday; E. Monday; F. 28

Page 84

A. scale; B. ruler; C. thermometer; D. cup; E. ruler; F. thermometer; G. ruler, H. cup

Page 85

A. 5; B. 1; C. 3; D. 4; E. 6; F. 4

Page 86

A. 13; B. 9; C. 12; D. 5; E. 10; F. 3; G. 6

Answer Key

Unit 6 Test

1. C; 2. A; 3. B; 4. D; 5. D;
6. B; 7. D; 8. C; 9. A; 10. C;
11. D; 12. A; 13. B; 14. D;
15. C; 16. A; 17. B; 18. A;
19. C; 20. B; Constructed-
response answers will vary.

Page 92

A. 5; B. 8; C. 13; D. horses;
E. pigs; F. sheep; G. hens
and cows

Page 93

A. 7 + 5 = 12; B. 8 − 5 = 3;
C. 3 + 6 = 9; D. 7 − 6 = 1;
E. 8; F. corn, G. 5; H. peas

Page 94

A. Fran; B. Fran; C. Franky;
D. 3; E. 5; F. 10; G. Fred
and Flip; H. 1

Page 95

A. Monday; B. Wednesday;
C. 5 + 3 = 8; D. 5 − 3 = 2;
E. 7 + 5 + 4 = 16; F.
Monday; G. Tuesday; H.
Wednesday

Page 96

Page 97

A. 1/2, B. 1/3, C. 2/4, D. 1/3,
E. 1/2, F. 3/4, G. 3/4, H. 2/3,
I. 1/2

Page 98

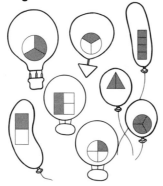

Page 99

Check students' pages.

Unit 7 Test

1. D; 2. A; 3. D; 4. B; 5. C;
6. B; 7. A; 8. B; 9. A; 10. C;
11. D; 12. C; 13. C; 14. A;
15. B; 16. D; 17. D; 18. D;
19. B; 20. C; Constructed
response: Bar graphs will
vary.

Page 105

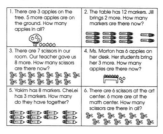

Page 106

A. 12 + 6 = 18; B. 8 + 7 =
15; C. 41 + 13 = 54; D. 21 +
15 = 36; E. 27 + 20 = 47;
F. 34 + 32 = 66; G. 51 + 32
= 83; H. 6 + 5 = 11

Page 107

1. Juan has 8 coins. He trades 4 of them away. How many are left?	2. Corey has 10 coins. He lost 3 of them. How many does he have left?
☒☒☒☒⊙⊙⊙⊙	☒☒☒⊙⊙⊙⊙⊙⊙⊙
3. Darby has 13 coins. She trades 5 of them away. How many are left?	4. Mei Lee has 6 coins. She gives 2 of them away. How many does she have now?
☒☒☒☒☒⊙⊙⊙⊙⊙⊙⊙⊙	☒☒⊙⊙⊙⊙
5. Mark has 11 coins. He lost 6. How many coins does Mark have now?	6. Denell has 12 coins. He gives 6 a them to a friend. How many are left?
☒☒☒☒☒☒⊙⊙⊙⊙⊙	☒☒☒☒☒☒⊙⊙⊙⊙⊙⊙
7. Margarite has 5 coins. She gives 2 to her sister. How many does she have now?	8. Shanise has 9 coins. She lost 4 on her way to school. How many does she have now?
☒☒⊙⊙⊙	☒☒☒☒⊙⊙⊙⊙⊙

Page 108

1. How many more, 67 − 45
= 22; B. difference, 89 − 23
= 57; C. difference, 99 − 67
= 32; D. will be left, 67 − 13
= 54; E. How many more, 89
− 20 = 69

Page 109

A. How much more, 78 − 42
= 36¢; B. in all, 21 + 21 =
42¢; C. altogether, 55 + 42 =
97¢; D. How much more, 78
− 55 = 23¢; E. total, 42 + 34
= 76¢;
F. difference, 78 − 34 = 44¢

Page 110

A. 99 − 78 = 21¢; B. 78 + 21
= 99¢; C. 67 − 34 = 33¢; D.
93 − 42 = 51¢; E. 55 + 21 =
76¢; F. 55 + 34 = 89¢; G. 83
− 42 = 41¢; H. 88 − 78 =
10¢

Page 111

A. 12 − 7 = 5; B. 14 + 14 =
28; C. 3 + 3 = 6; D. 8 + 5 =
13; E. 12 − 8 = 4; F. 18 − 9 =
9

Page 112

8, 5

Unit 8 Test

1. B; 2. D; 3. A; 4. C; 5. B;
6. A; 7. B; 8. D; 9. B; 10. D;
11. C; 12. B; 13. D; 14. B;
15. B; 16. D; 17. A; 18. A;
19. C; 20. C; Constructed-
response answers will vary.

Final Review Test

1. D; 2. A; 3. B; 4. D; 5. A;
6. C; 7. B; 8. A; 9. B; 10. C;
11. A; 12. C; 13. D; 14. A;
15. B; 16. C; 17. C; 18. B;
19. B; 20. A; 21. D; 22. D;
23. A; 24. A; 25. B; 26. D;
27. B; 28. C; 29. D; 30. B;
Constructed response:
78−34 = 44, Answers will
vary.